Hype Praise for
3 American Cranks

"If you read just one book this year... you're doing better than most college graduates."
    -- Anonymous

"It made me laugh."
    -- F. Nietzsche

"Brilliant... a work of genius. Should be up for a Pulitzer."
    -- Author's Mother

"Better he should get a real job for once in his life."
    -- Author's Father

"If your idea of heaven is settling down with a good book -- get a life!"
    -- Name Withheld

"He who judges a work by its testimonial quotes is bound to be reading an oxcart load of pretty disappointing books."
    -- Confucius or Lao-Tzu. Take your pick.

"If you could bring just one book on a desert island... don't you think it should be *How to Survive on a Desert Island*?"
    -- Author of *How to Survive on a Desert Island*

"You've stood in this bookstore reading free stuff for more than an hour now. I'm calling Security."
    -- The Manager

3 AMERICAN CRANKS

3 American Cranks

A Satire in Three Voices

by

R. L. Feliciello

PazziBoy Press
New York

This work is a product of the author's imagination. Any resemblance herein to persons living or dead is purely coincidental.

Text and cover design copyright © 2016 by R. L. Feliciello

All rights reserved under International and Pan-American Copyright Conventions. No part of this book may be used or reproduced in any manner whatsoever without prior written permission of the author, except in the case of brief quotations embodied in critical articles and reviews.

Published by PazziBoy Press, New York

First Edition, April 2016

Cover graphics and author photo: www.konboogie.com

Library of Congress Control Number 2016904943

ISBN 978-0-9974117-0-6

Also available in hardcover

To the better angels of our nature.

Satire
\'sa-ti(e)r\
[L. *satira*, full plate, medley, *satis* enough, also see SAD]
A literary form in prose or verse utilizing a blend of wit, irony, and humor that exposes as laughable a particular idea, vice, personal folly or institution, including government and society, for the purposes of betterment and entertainment.

CONTENTS

1.

Trialogue 1	Hello and Hello Einstein Never Wore Socks This Wifeless Planet	3
Trialogue 2	Vice President of the United States Conjugal Visits The Elect and The Elected	17
Trialogue 3	Secret Love Queen of the Laundromat The Formula for Success	29
Trialogue 4	Into the Maëlstrom The Wrong House by Mistake The Only Rigid Body in Nature	45

2.

Trialogue 5	The American ZZ-ZZ Fly A Blonde and a Banknote Master, Eat	57
Trialogue 6	What Is She Thinking Right Now? A Moderately Large Idaho Potato Aunt Bertha's Toes	73
Trialogue 7	Hail, Realdo Colombo Where's My White Rabbit? Rule, Britannia!	85
Trialogue 8	Glittering Indifference Find a Nice Man King Me!	95

3.

Trialogue 9	500,000 Applicants Jesus's Goat Is the Lord Your Shepherd?	111
Trialogue 10	When An American Prays Philistia Is Just Over the Hill A Bull and a Bullfinch	125
Trialogue 11	Leave Your Bootstraps Alone The Things That Are Caesar's The Index of Covetability	133
Trialogue 12	This Barren Autogamy I'm Staying Right Here Declare Your Independence	145

1.

Trialogue 1

Hello and Hello
Einstein Never Wore Socks
This Wifeless Planet

Hello and hello, my fellow slaves. We used to pick cotton. Now we pick dollars. My name is D. C. Washington, and I cannot tell a lie. The Constitution says there shall be neither slavery nor involuntary servitude, and yet we're all slaves of the dollar. Is the United States of America unConstitutional?

I'M NOBODY'S SLAVE.

Excuse me, Sir, but I see you're wearing your shackle here this morning. The necktie is the new shackle. You don't know you're a slave because they've got you confused. You're a member of the Muddled Class. Today's shackle is made of silk instead of iron, and you wear it around your neck instead of your ankle, but it works just the same. They've got you so confused you go out and buy your own shackle.

I WORKED MY WAY UP TO WHERE I AM.

Let me ask you this, Sir, if I may. Do you own your own home?

YES, I DO.

And you still don't know you're a slave? There, I got him smiling. He knows I'm telling the truth. My name is D. C. Washington, and I cannot tell a lie.

But isn't it just like the Muddled Class to think just because they own a mortgage and the other fellow doesn't that they're more free than the other guy? They think just because they turn their paycheck over to the bank every month that they're not a slave and the other fellow is. Isn't that just the house slave calling the field slave black?

Today it's not the black man who's the slave. It's the Muddled Class, but they don't know it. At least the black man knew he was a slave back then. The black man has declared his Independence. He no longer cottons, but you poor Muddled Class fellows are confused. When the Great Depression hit here a while back you didn't see any black folks jumping out of high windows, did you? No. Because they knew the score you can't buy in the store that the Business of America is not Business. You don't see me wearing the shiny silk shackle of the Muddled Class. I'm not blaming you Muddled Class fellows, you understand. I sympathize with you. Why do you think I take the trouble to address you here on the steps of this Memorial to my distant relative, Thomas Jefferson, in all kinds of weather, whether there's one person or two hundred people on the steps to listen to me? I say I sympathize with you. I want to help you in my own small way as sort of a home-style missionary, not your usual kind of Christian mercenary that travels far afield to carry the blessings of American Mammonization overseas. My humble ministry is right here with you. The Lord is my Shepherd. I shall not want. Not only do I "shall not want," I *do* not want. The fellow in the White House may be my President, but the Lord is my Shepherd.

HEY, D. C.?

Yes, young man?

CAN I ASK YOU A QUESTION?

Of course, my friend. Go right ahead.

WHAT DOES D. C. STAND FOR?

District of Columbia. What's the matter with you? Aren't you educated? You went through the entire Muddled Class school system and you didn't learn an important thing like that? You should have gone to one of our separate but equal black schools. That's where you learn things. Take the District of Columbia, for example. Why was the District of Columbia named after Christopher Columbus? I'll tell you why. Because the Congress is here, and every time the Congress tries to get somewhere it ends up someplace else entirely, just like Columbus. The Congress keeps setting out for the Promised Land, and all we get landed with is the same ole U.S.A.

YOU DON'T SOUND 100% AMERICAN TO ME.

Excuse me, who is that who is casting aspersions upon my percentage of Americanness?

ME. I DID.

Now, Ma'am, aren't I black? And isn't the black man the only 100% American? The black man is the only 100% American because all you folks, every one of you, you or your forefathers and foremothers, came to this country to better your lot. The black man is the only one who came to this country to make his lot worse. That's how much the black man loves this country. Not even the *statue* of Liberty was waiting for the black man when his ship pulled in. Some say the black man is shiftless and lazy and doesn't want to work. But, remember, the black man came to this country to try to keep it honest, and that's a full-time job. We're working round the clock, and it's hard work, too. I'll say it again. The black man is the only 100% American.

D. C., YOU HAVE TO ADMIT THEY GAVE MARTIN LUTHER KING HIS OWN DAY.

Yes, they did. It is fitting that we honor Doctor King but more important that we value what he stood for -- not just racial but economic justice, and being wary of trigger-happy politicians. There's only one thing that concerns me when they give a man his own day. Sometimes they give a man a day so they can ignore his teachings the rest of the year. Well, It worked with Christmas, didn't it?

YOU SAY THE BLACK MAN IS THE ONLY 100% AMERICAN. WHAT ABOUT THE INDIANS?

Oh, now, I was doing you a favor by not bringing up the red man. The red man will always be prior to any talk of who is and who is not 100% American. The red man is like the God of the Old Testament who said, "I am who I am." Before Abraham Lincoln was, he was. The red man will always be prior to any percentage of Americanness. I would say that the red man loves this country even more than the black man, if that's possible. The black man came here to find some lack of Opportunity, and we were lucky, we found ours as soon as they shoved us down the gangplank. But the red man had to come here and then wait twelve or thirteen thousand years.

The red man was here before any of us, but the red man was being very unBusinesslike. During the time he occupied this prime real estate all by himself he did not leave behind one major highway, not one big city, nothing to speak of in the way of an opera house or orchestra suitable for weddings.

The red man was letting the place go to seed. The white man crossed the ocean to save this country from complete ruination. It was a good thing the white man walked on water to get here. Why, if it wasn't for the white man, we wouldn't have any National Parks in this country. Try to imagine this great country without one single National Park. Not only no National Parks, but no city parks, either. Where was a man supposed to walk his dog? You see the problem.

I hold these truths to be self-evident and obvious. And so, my fellow slaves, as I go among you now hat in hand to receive your kind donations to my ministry, please repeat after me.

O, Overloads.

O, OVERLORDS.

I will be a good slave.

I WILL BE A GOOD SLAVE.

Come on now. *All* of you. You, too, please, Ma'am. No one gets away free here:
I will be a good slave.

I WILL BE A GOOD SLAVE.

Good. Thank you. Nice and loud now so my distant relative can hear you:
I will spend my life picking dollars.

I WILL SPEND MY LIFE PICKING DOLLARS.

Till death or taxes do us part.

TILL DEATH OR TAXES DO US PART.

Beautiful. I thank you all for participating in my little service and hope to see you right here on these steps again, lunchtime tomorrow. Go in peace, brothers and sisters, and thank you for supporting my little ministry.

D. C.?

Yes, young lady? By the way, I'm curious. Are you two together, you and the young man beside you?

NO. NO, WE'RE NOT TOGETHER.

Look at them both shaking their heads. Well, I think you'd make a very good couple. What do you think, folks? Yes, I'll applaud that, too.

I'm sorry, Miss, you had a question?

I'LL BE GLAD TO DONATE TO YOUR MINISTRY, BUT WHAT ABOUT THE LILIES OF THE FIELD?

Birds would be appreciated, but currency is needed.

I MEAN THE BIBLE SAYS WE SHOULDN'T CONCERN OURSELVES WITH MONEY BUT BEHOLD THE LILIES OF THE FIELD.

Yes, behold the lilies of the field, for they sow not, neither do they reap, but neither do they have to pay rent or luxury tax. And what happened to the lilies when they covered over the field to put in a parking lot? The Good Book doesn't say a thing about that.

I know, I know, Prosperity is just around the corner. But there's a wolf between me and the corner. Times is *hard*.

. . .

Anyone, especially a female, who attempts a bold reinterpretation of the world on a scientific basis is going to find there is no room at the inn. That is to be expected. People do not care to know the truth about their world, because the laws of matter are not mundane. The laws of matter are the spirit of the universe. What can my landlady possibly know of the joys of undertaking investigations of the utmost importance? Why does she suppose I have taken upon myself the work that I have begun? Not because I love logic and mathematics. Logic and mathematics bore me. It is not a case of what one wants to do in life, of what one is *good* at. If Einstein had only applied himself in mathematics, there is no telling what he might have accomplished.

We are, every one of us, subject to all five dimensions. I know that now. I tried to skip steps. That's when I became ill, and the rumor spread that I had undergone electroshock therapy. I was hospitalized for *exhaustion*. They have decided that depression is a disease. What they call depression is, in a great mind, merely an invitation to profound philosophical investigation. My father is always telling me to smile. People! They wag their finger at you and call you depressed unless you're constantly airing your teeth. Ours is a nation of boosters and brightsiders, from whom may God deliver me.

To call my landlady simply mediocre would be an act of compassion positively Jesusian. She has to throw her head back like a sword swallower to see mediocrity. She burns incense in her bathroom. She uses it as an air freshener! That's the mentality exactly. The woman has reached a level of mindlessness unmatched since the Stone Age, or just the stone. When I told her I was troubled by nightmares, she said, "Maybe you should get back in touch with your analyst." She pretends not to be aware of their suicide rate. They dive only as deep as the unconscious then get the bends and have to come up for air. How can they be expected to understand? A person capable of uttering the words, "Maybe you should get back in touch with your analyst," is incapable of understanding anything of the utmost importance. She is typical of this city and she's not the only one. "We don't have any carrots to sell." The greengrocer actually said that to me. And the minute you mention Wittgenstein, their eyes roll back in their heads.

I have been dealt a blow but I'm not going to let that woman put me out on the street. My work is too important. I will take all the steps. Just as the Virgin Mary did. I used to think that the Virgin Mary was simply the worse case on record of a mother who had ruined her son's chances for a normal life. I know better now. I know what Mary went through. Do you think I need a man to conceive a child in me? I've learned the mathematics involved.

I overheard my landlady complaining to her friend about me. "Look at that bed. Look. Look. The blanket thrown over the mattress without a sheet. That's the way an escaped convict would make a bed. Where are the sheets I supplied her out of my own bounty? Look at the window wide open in the middle of winter. Look at this, the pillow without the pillowcase. Is that the way a civilized person lives? I'll have to have this room fumigated the minute she's out of here. Oh, my God. The sheets crumpled up in a corner of the closet. Eee! She's going to pay for this. I'm going to send her father a bill. I'm going to itemize a bill and send it to him. She doesn't eat. That's her problem. She lives on water for a week, and then I find things missing from my refrigerator. None of my other boarders do that. You wouldn't find any of my other girls stealing food. She goes to the kitchen in the middle of the night and eats my leftovers. I've seen her in a corner in the dark chomping on a chicken leg like a savage. I can't take this another day. This is my house! This is my home! She refuses to talk to me now. She slides the rent under the door in a sealed envelope, like a ransom note. There is food missing from my refrigerator. Food I clearly labeled! Things I was planning to have for lunch the next day. I want her out of here. I don't care who her father is. Plenty of decent-living girls inquire after my rooms every day. She refuses to wear underthings. When I politely mentioned the subject to her, do you know what she had the nerve to tell me? Without blinking an eye she stood there and said, 'Einstein never wore socks.' Is that any way to talk? Is that a normal person talking? She's got gorgeous, raven-black hair that reaches to the small of her back. But no, it's not black. It's blonde. She dyes it. I've seen the roots in the clump of hairs clogging the shower drain. She showers four-five times a day. I show her the water bill and she stares into space. She's such a beautiful young woman. She has one blue eye and one green eye, one more stunning than the other. And she uses them to stare into space. You don't know what it does to me to see a beautiful young woman like that staring into space."

Yes, I stare into space. But my staring is of a higher order. When she stares into space she sees – nothing. That is the difference between us. "Maybe you should get back in touch with your analyst." Not those alienists. They're not fooling anyone. People are on to their game. Their fifty minutes are up. Do you suppose this moral chaos can go on much longer? I will never again give my trust to the Republican Party. For an American, that's nadir's bedrock. I will never give up my work. They say I was born fist first. I have known the fourth dimension. Doorknobs come off in my hand!

. . .

I can't hold on much longer. I've got to get some relief soon. I've been dragging myself around this wifeless planet for nineteen years now. In nineteen years I haven't once experienced a vaginal orgasm. This is serious. Youth is the springtime of life. I'm in the seedtime of youth. And it's all going to waste. All this caterwauling in the dark and no neck well bitten into. Romeo and Juliet were married and dead by my age.

SO CLOSE

> I could die.
> There's no telling what might happen.
> I might be struck by a truck,
> And hear my neck go snappin'.
>
> Where is my wife?
> Where my proud paternity?
> It's hard to live so far from love
> And so close to eternity.

I may be only nineteen years old but I've learned a thing or two. I've learned that I am not a rational being. I am my *membrum virilum*. I'm not six foot four. I'm a mere two inches, give or take one and a half.

I've learned that only three things exist on this planet. They are me, women who induce vasocongestion, and everything else. I throb with intentions, all day long. I can't help it. It's in my blood, from way back. God threw Adam a bone and said, "Fetch." Adam went bounding through the tall grass, tongue aflap, in drooling pursuit of that far-flung os. I understand the Genesis of my predicament, but that doesn't help. This wild, thrashing Garden hose. I can't hold on much longer. I've heard of the tail wagging the dog, but this is ridiculous. Whenever I see a luscious young female, my testicles fly out to her like the bola of an Argentine gaucho. At the sight of a tumefacient female hope springs forth from my person. What I want to know is -- Is this love or just the next generation trying to get out? It's embarrassingly automatic. If she's pubescent, I'm tumescent. One moment it's Florida, the next the Blue Ridge Mountains. Are varicose veins normal for a person my age?

I'm being held captive in a four-hole laughing stock, and that hurts. I get so downhearted. This is not your ordinary Saturday evening post-. I'm talking about *non*coital depression. I read that coupling dogs sometimes become locked in the mating position. Some Chihuahuas are doing better than I am.

Why am I being this way? Why can't I look at life on a higher plane? Is it because the children of the great are doomed to suffer? My father is the most prominent gynecologist in Washington, D.C. All the V.I.P. wives visit his clinic. What's left for me to aspire to? Every day, mothers bring their daughters to him and ask him to stare fixedly at their downy betweenleggedness. Can anything top that? It's going to make accountancy seem dull by comparison.

    When I see a girl like that one with the ponytail, skating by on one foot, my sexual organ begins to feel like an aviary for fireflies. I hear about guys vacationing with their sweethearts down in Rio de Janeiro and Puerto Vallarta. I'd like to spend two weeks with her in Flagrante Delicto. Hymens are like platform promises, aren't they? This very evening we could be sharing love and intermingling smegma. Is that wrong? I want to plunge my hope into her charity. I want us to share that moment beyond time when os meets os and, os to os, we fly together up to paradise. I'd like to send her a spray of baby's breath. We could achieve simultaneous carpopedal spasm. And, when all is said and done that could be said and done, I'll roll over, rest my head beside hers on the pillow, and ask if there's any leftover chicken in the refrigerator. I'm positive it goes on every night in every house on every block in this city.

Trialogue 2

Vice President of the United States
Conjugal Visits
The Elect and The Elected

"Your father loves you," my landlady says. She says that because she's been F.B.I.-ing my mail. She saw the check his accountant sends every two weeks. Of course she knows who my father is. Would I have been allowed to remain in this house this long if she were not so impressed that my father came this close to being named a candidate for the vice presidency? Vice president of the United States. An honorable man would rather be right than president and anything than vice president. But not father. He still hopes to get the call this time around. But there will be no hope for the Republican Party at the polls this election unless the Chairman of the Republican National Committee reads and acts on the letter I sent him. I made everything very clear, very explicit.

Vice president. I can't get over it. Vice president, occupier of the Offal Office. John Adams loathed the job. Aaron Burr murdered Alexander Hamilton for making him vice president. My father calls me an egghead. That dunce. He couldn't spell I.Q. with an unabridged dictionary. Father doesn't have a mind. He has a mentality. He is living in an era. He is hopelessly limited. He criticizes me for listening to jazz. He described jazz as a group of black musicians in a drugged up frenzy trying to finish a three-minute song in twelve minutes.

He tried to match me up with a Secret Service man on the chance that it might somehow put his name one more time in front of the powers that be at Party headquarters. What can you say of a father who would push his daughter at a Secret Service man? The Secret Service -- they're so absurd in their dark glasses and business suits – part hardened criminal, part well-dressed professional, the fusing of pathological murderer with his defense attorney. One of them invited me to fly with him to Las Vegas for the weekend. Las Vegas, where there once was a desert, they brought forth a wasteland.

My father says he wants respect. He doesn't want respect, he wants deference. Call no man father upon earth. Jesus wrote those words in red ink for a reason. In ancient times the father was free to have his child sold into slavery or abandoned on a mountainside. Today the father has fallen into a funk because he must settle for breaking the child's will over the knee of property. "Get that ashtray away from the baby!" Does he think I don't remember!

We live in a post-patriarchal age. The Right of the Father is dead. But the male is not dead, only wounded. And like a wounded animal he fights, struggling against his lost hegemony. From city to city he wanders, the urban nomad, in search of a higher paying job, foraging for fame, scampering for status, pilfering for prestige. He's trying to earn respect with the things he can buy. You see him every day on the sidewalk with his store-bought confidence, store-bought pride, store-bought dignity. For the Pursuit of Happiness, read the Pursuit of Property. For the Pursuit of Property, read the pursuit of power. But it's no use. His time has passed. His fate is sealed. His fortune is told. You hear a lot of talk about a man making his fortune. One does not make one's fortune. One's fortune makes one. One may make money, but that is another matter altogether.

. . .

I want a woman right now. She doesn't have to be all that young. If she's between menstruation and menopause, that's fine. Where is the nurse when you really need her? This is another instance of how the health care system in this country has let us down. The government should do more. I've spent many a frustrating afternoon in the Senate gallery waiting for the introduction of that special piece of legislation mandating that every young American, male and female, spend the summers of his or her thirteenth to nineteenth years in one of twelve dozen federally funded Youth Nooky Camps to be set up within our natural wilderness areas. There each young person would be required by law to take part in a full round of activities designed to pique natural sexual feeling and expression -- healthy exercises and games, such as ducks and drakes, nude tongue wrestling, and bobbing for nipples. Such a piece of legislation is not likely to pass both the House and the Senate. And they wonder why young people are apathetic about politics.

    Why am I being this way? The other night I was sitting front row center at the piano recital of a virginal prodigy from Sweden at her début performance. All during her first piece I kept imagining myself as *Primo Uomo* performing Opus Number One, in C minor, *pianissimo con molto tenerezza*. What is wrong with me?

              STEINWAY & SONS
        Swede vulviform cunny,
        Blonde and pink as a bunny,

You make my globe sunny.
I'm the bear, you're the honey.
Frédéric Chopin and Georgina Sand.

I wonder if my parents would allow conjugal visits in my room. How could they understand what I'm going through? They have never had sex. As I understand the matter it requires a certain degree of passion. The only passions I've seen them surrender to are ennui and condescension.

Maybe I'm misjudging them. Maybe they would understand my plight. But I'm terrified that, if I open my mouth on the subject, they'll kick me out without a penny. What of it? I could take off to the South Pacific. I read about a great job in the Philippines where they pay a guy to go from village to village deflowering virgins. We don't have good jobs like that in this country. I know. I've scoured the classifieds.

Actually, I don't really believe there is a job in the Philippines deflowering virgins. If there were why would so many young Filipino men join the U.S. Navy?

I can't stop thinking about a girl who was standing next to me the other day on the steps of the Jefferson Memorial. Not a girl, a young woman, a brunette sporting black-plastic, movie-star sunglasses. Very striking. No makeup at all, her forehead scrubbed shiny. When she slipped off her glasses to ask D. C. Washington a question,

I saw that she has one blue eye and one green eye. Overwhelmed by that burst of color I felt like a bee suddenly cured of blindness seeing a flower for the first time. The flower was saying, "Here's the nectar. Come get the nectar. It's very nice nectar, top quality nectar." Then the flower put her dark glasses back on.

. . .

My name is D. C. Washington, and I cannot tell a lie. I love living in Washington because I love presidential elections. I love them because they give the impression power is changing hands. Why they give that impression I have no idea. Power hasn't changed fingers in thousands of years. What makes us think it's going to change hands the first Tuesday in November?

The Elect and the Elected, that's what it's come down to. Our forefathers brought forth upon this continent a generation of men dedicated to making our government work. Today our politicians have dedicated themselves to *getting* government work. Our Constitution says we shall be protected from cruel and unusual punishments, and yet we have to pay the salaries of senators and congressmen. Is the United States of America unConstitutional?

As a people we Americans don't put much stock in our politicians. It's a tradition with us. It goes all the way back to our Founding Fathers. Oh, yes. In the Constitution where they're counting people for purposes of representation in the Congress, they set it down that it takes five black men to make three human beings, but it takes 30,000 human beings to make one congressman.

Our politicians have an important job to do. It's true. Their job is to keep Business honest. Who keeps the politicians honest? The newspapers. Who keeps the newspapers honest? The fellow who writes letters to the editor. Who keeps that guy honest? Nobody. That's the beauty of the thing. Nobody is accountable, so we can all keep counting. Well, filling pockets is our national pastime, isn't it?

Actually, no, no, that's not true. In a democracy the voter keeps everybody honest. He keeps the newspapers honest by writing letters to the editor, as I said, and he keeps the politician honest, too. As soon as he finds out, from the newspaper, that some politician is working under the Check and Balances system – that's where the politician says to the Interests, "As long as the Check Balances it's okay by me" – that fellow is voted out of office, so some other fellow can take his place in the Check and Balances system. Isn't that a good system?

They tell me we live in a democracy, and I believe them. But don't it seem that democracy is just doughocracy with a press agent? It used to be King Cotton. Now it's King Currency. We're living under the Money Monarchs. These big money kings of the banks and the rest, they don't think much of the public, you know. But they don't seem to mind public money coming their way.

I hate to be unBusinesslike, but there are people right now in this country who don't have enough to eat, whose nerves are shattered, who may be out of luck entirely, due to a certain allergy to doctor bills. If they don't do something soon down the street in Congress to spread around some prosperity, all that talk about a car in every garage and a chicken in every pot is going to change. There's going to be a chicken in every garage, and you're going to have to decide whether to eat it or ride *it* into town. Of course, I believe we ought to give the next President a chance to prove himself, but he'd better do something fast or there may be terrible times ahead, and not just for the poor folks. You've heard about going from log cabin to White House? Well, it can go in the opposite direction, too. If things don't improve soon, there's going to be a log cabin where the White House is now.

You know as well as I do this governmentlessness has got to stop. We all sense that. Now, I'm not saying the government has to do everything for us. We learned a long time ago there's no Great White Father in Washington. The government is more like an uncle. He might care about you but he's not responsible. He might be sympathetic but he doesn't want to get deeply involved. He's just the uncle.

Don't fall for that old Great White Father routine. The last ones to fall for that haven't seen a buffalo since Taft was president.

D. C.?

Yes, Sir, the gentleman waving his hand in the air.

WOULD YOU SAY WE HAVE A REPUBLICAN OR A DEMOCRATIC FORM OF GOVERNMENT?

Some days I can't see any form to it at all. They tell me we live in a democracy, and I believe them. But isn't a democracy a place where nothing happens to you in a government way without your consent? Now, do you remember being asked whether you wanted your income taxed? I know my memory isn't what it used to be, but would somebody please tell me which day it was we were asked to vote on that? Could be I was sick the day we voted that in. I can't remember.

My grandfather was old enough to remember reading in the newspapers back in 1917: AMERICA DECLARES WAR ON GERMANY! He told me he did not recall voting on that. Of course, that war was fought for a noble cause, the War to end all *Warts*.

Thousands and thousands of our young boys sent over there never had to worry about warts again. So that was a good thing. But did the mothers and fathers of those boys vote on that? My grandfather told me he didn't remember voting on that, but then his memory failed him something awful toward the end.

We have in our country a one-man, one-vote rule – down the street in Congress, that is. We little guys don't vote. We vote for the voters, then the voters vote. We are a Christian and democratic nation – Christian on Sunday and democratic in November.

WHO'S GOING TO WIN THE NEXT WAR?

What's wrong with you? Don't you have a mind to buy with? Don't you have a late-model automobile to think with? Don't you give credence to what you hear on the news? The good guys are going to win. The good guys always win, or what's the point of getting involved in such a hellish business? When the smoke clears, if it ever does clear next time around, we'll know who the good guys are. They might be us. They might be the other guys. You can never be too sure when it comes to how a war is going to end up.

War winning and ending have become very iffy nowadays. Peace only seems to last as long as it takes to raise up a new crop of patriots. You all know what a peace treaty is. A peace treaty is a triumph of diplomacy where all the big nations sit down and solemnly swear to stay out of war until the next opportunity.

Tell me if I'm wrong, but isn't war just Abraham and Isaac all over again? Except this time Abraham issues Isaac a uniform, which doesn't fit, and there's no Angel. You red-bloodied American boys, you know how to get your blood even redder, don't you? You shed it. Oh, but it won't have been shed for nothing, exactly. We'll be thinking of you every year during our Memorial Day picnic. Are the hotdogs ready yet? Hey, did anybody remember to bring the mustard?

I don't blame the soldiers. I'm a veteran myself and proud of it. It's the only job I was ever recruited for. Oh, yes, I'm a member of that great and venerable organization, the Veterans of Foreign Defense Actions. Seems we'll defend our shores even if we have to go halfway around the world to find them. My only problem with those war-boosting veterans' organizations is they limit membership to the survivors. We never get to hear from the other fellows.

MISTER WASHINGTON?

Yes, Sir, there in the back, with the bowtie.

THANK YOU.

You're welcome.

ARE YOU SAYING YOU DON'T BELIEVE IN A JUST WAR?

Well, really, I do have a problem with that. Because, as far as I can make out, a just war means that it's bad for Cain to kill Abel, but it's a swell thing for Abel to kill Cain all the day long.

And, you know, they send our boys Over There for reasons they don't understand too clearly. All they are made to understand is that if they don't go off to whatever foreign country Cain happens to live in at the time, they're a coward who would rather hold the door of his house open so heathen savages can butcher his kindly old grandmother, his about-to-give-birth wife, and his two and a half peacefully sleeping children who only a moment before dozed off with the final words of a bedtime story faintly echoing in their ears. Of course, we don't have but one or two cowards of that sort in the whole country.

To be honest with you, what I've seen in my humble lifetime is that war is nothing but Cain, Incorporated. They say the Marines are our bravest men because they're the first ones there when the trouble starts. But I would say the Business Man is even braver because, nine times out of ten, wasn't he there even before the trouble started?

Trialogue 3

Secret Love
The Queen of the Laundromat
The Formula for Success

Be gentle. Be understanding. Your parents are getting old. Seeing death approach, how could you add insult to The Final Injury? Oh, so advanced age confers amnesty for all past crimes? Because they have death on their side they can get away with absolutely anything? They control you with fear until the day you finally outgrow fear, then comes the plea for sympathy. Then they roll in the sarcophagus. They leave it in the center of the living room and crouch behind it, now and then lobbing over accusations of ingratitude.

"Your parents are getting old," my landlady says. "Old people can't take those kinds of shocks." Of course, they're getting old. It's their own fault. They have made themselves old. Those people have eaten stockyard after stockyard of red meat and then they wonder why they're getting old. Did Einstein age? Did Bertrand Russell age? Did Socrates? Did Christ?

Mother expects me to come around to him for a deathbed reconciliation. There will be no deathbed reconciliation. I've tried to sit down and talk with him civilly. I have. I showed up at his office one morning. His secretary stood up from her desk and tried to treat me like one of his constituents, but I walked right past her. A reporter and a photographer were in there with him, but father dismissed them. He offered me a chair. I sat down. We passed polite words back and forth, but nothing was said.

And mother goes right along with him. Women like her, in their ignorance and fright, keep the whole edifice in place. Devoted wives! Loyal caryatids supporting the sacred temple of androcracy -- all for their man, that insufferable braggart masquerading as The Patriarch. I don't know what would have become of me if I hadn't gone away to boarding school. The boarding school is the institution that, nearly alone, accounts for the success of the higher orders in breeding men and women of poise and accomplishment. It affords the growing child the opportunity to learn masturbation away from the stultifying influence of her parents.

"He loves you, dear. He just doesn't feel it." Those are mother's exact words. I've tried to reason with her but she is lost, paralyzed. She can't see the forest fire for the trees. Once, during a fast that I carried on too long, I spelled out, across the full-length triptych mirror in their bedroom -- with a fingertip and my own blood -- Proverbs 27:5, Open rebuke is better than secret love. Did she understand? Did she get the message? No. She took it as the sign of a complete nervous collapse.

Last summer I spoke to her for four hours on the phone from London. I said it all. I was very explicit. I found the precise formulation that could not be refuted. A week later she calls me in Palm Springs and grills me for not sending him a Father's Day card. How do I make her understand that there are certain sentiments that cannot be adequately expressed in greeting card verse? "Oh, missy, I thought you had got all that out of your system. You mustn't be so sensitive, dear." Oh, my God!

Mother keeps reminding me of his heart condition, says I'm slowly killing him. Good God, doesn't he finally have to take some responsibility, if only for his own death? It matters little if he goes to his grave tomorrow or twenty tomorrows from now. But, for God's sake, let him get there on his own two feet.

She says I broke his heart when I refused to attend my debutante ball. So, he's still holding that against me. Is it my fault he is incapable of appreciating that going off to the desert as I did was a much greater coming-of-age than any taffeta cow auction? How many of those fine young ladies would have dared live sixteen days out of reach of their perfumed double-ply? How many could have slept under the stars with only the cold, blue Coachella Valley sky for blanket? I would have stayed longer, but I began experiencing blackouts after the second week. It was 115 degrees, and a fire in the mountains was sending up an apocalypse of ash. But I learned something. I learned that you cannot skip steps. In the work that I am doing that becomes more and more evident.

All I can accuse him of is heartlessness, but he charges me with ingratitude. Why does that carry more weight, even with me? I'm standing there with blood under my nails, seeing scratches on his face. But, call the ambulance. He has snapped a cold pike from off his icicled heart, and I am run through. No, Your Honor, I cannot produce the murder weapon. It has melted in the heat of his denials.

He is not my true father. My true father died by his own hand when I was four years old. He carried one of his double-barrel shotguns to his library and applied his brain to a leather-bound set of *The Complete Correspondence of Gottfried Wilhelm von Leibniz*. He had been working on the Law of Large Numbers. His last act, before going for the shotgun, was to set fire to his mathematical manuscripts in the enormous fireplace of the main house on the Cape. Bernhard Riemann had laid the mathematical groundwork for Einstein to build upon. Riemann made Einstein possible. I have had to work alone all these years. I remember well the night my father fed that fire. I was supposed to be upstairs asleep. The whole state of Massachusetts was asleep. But from my room I heard quiet sobbing downstairs. I left my bed and, with my porcelain doll for protection, stepped out pajamaed and barefoot to the landing. I could see him down there through the open door of his library, placing page after page on the fire, careful to pull his hand away from the flames, as if he still valued his life. That was the last time I saw his face, except at the funeral. On the way back from the cemetery I squeezed myself into a corner of the back seat, fingered the curls of my porcelain doll, and wondered whether he would have made that fire if he had had a son.

. . .

There are three kinds of females: the kind you can't have, the kind you don't really want, and the kind you end up with. Plain girls don't trigger my fantasies. A plain girl doesn't confer anything. I need a glossy woman, a woman with sheen. She's got to turn heads. I'm looking for the kind of female that turns heads, who, just walking along the sidewalk, could cause a traffic jam from here back to Henry Ford.

Why am I not attracted to girls as plain as an axiom in Euclid? I keep telling myself, Go for the plain girl. If she's plain I get along better with her. With a plain girl I can talk up a tornado. I tell myself, The pretty girl is nothing but trouble. The pretty girl is just the plain girl's revenge. But I receive stronger signals from women of heat. That's the way the equipment's made.

Wherever I happen to be I scan the females present and decide which is The Queen of that particular locale. She might be the Queen of the Laundromat, Queen of the Classroom, Queen of the Drugstore, Queen of the Elevator, Queen of the Dentist's Waiting Room, or, as is the case right now, Queen of the Beach on the Potomac on a hot summer day.

Look at that brunette in the yellow bikini. Why don't I go right over and ask her to let me write forbidden words with a tube of tanning cream between the parallel flesh lines of her rib cage? I'd like to take her to the outskirts of the city and force her to cook for me. But why do I long to perform the marriage act upon her? Can't Nature see we're both single?

Oh, and that blonde in the pink sitting on the pier, brushing her hair, and dangling freshly reddened toenails over the side. I know I could be happy with her, for twenty minutes. Observe the cool and serene demeanor. If she only knew that I am completely naked under this bathing suit, that supernatural naiad would throw off that bored and contemptuous mask, dive headfirst into the River of Desire, dog paddle to just below where I am standing, and implore me in water-gagged syllables to, quick, throw her a manrope.

Blonde hair! It is so attractive, so eye-catching. Blonde is Nature's neon. The blonde is human gold, and America is definitely on the gold standard. Any man who's never had a blonde, simply doesn't know the lay of the land. No American male can be quite sure of the richness of his sexual life until he's engaged in aural sex.

Look, now she's lying back sleepily sunning herself. With eyes shut to the envious world, she basks in her own radiant inheritance, as if the whole North American continent beneath her were her personal raft. Slender forearms lead the eye to tapered fingers resting, intertwined upon her navel. She turns over onto her stomach. I inch closer and see at the small of her back a tiny prairie fire of golden hairs. In plain English, a marriageable female.

The woman I marry must be an authentic All-Seven blonde gilded at each of these locations: scalp, eyebrows, lashes, areole, thighs, small of the back, and, of course, the *pièce de résistance*, the *mons veneris* (*vide infra*).

Now she's rolling onto her back again. Why doesn't she look my way? Should I yell out how much I admire the shape of her calves? How do I explain that I've fallen in love with the way she displaces air? I'm going to walk over to her, clear my throat, and simply admit I'm having trouble resisting the urge to use my sinister femoral artery to slip a studding-sail-tack-bend knot through her right obturator foramen. Or maybe not.

. . .

Let's let the cat out of the bag just a little bit. The poor little kitty is choking in there. Let's talk about our great American Mythfacts. You know what a Mythfact is, don't you?

NO, WHAT IS IT, D. C.?

Thank you, my friend. A Mythfact is like a big apple tree that doesn't bear fruit. It's only good for making shade that people can lay down under and fall asleep. You see, to get you where they want you, they have to first get you to fall asleep. How? By feeding you some good ole apple pie made from the same variety of apples eaten by Snow White in the fairytale. She was told that if she ate the apple her dream would come true. It's the same apple they've been feeding you all your life, because you have to be asleep before you can slip into that good ole American Dreaminess.

You've been enjoying that apple pie, you've swallowed it whole, and now you're feeling a little sleepy, aren't you? Your eyelids are getting heavy (you will go to college). Your eyelids are closing now (there will be lots of Opportunity waiting for you after you graduate). You feel very, very drowsy (ours is a Free to be Enterprising System where you can be as Enterprising as you please). You are now totally and completely asleep, the deepest, most profound sleep you've ever experienced. Awaking from this sleep you will feel free and confident, very optimistic, with not a care in the world. When I snap my fingers I want you to open your eyes. Snap! Okay now *buy something*!

In our country, three major Mythfacts reign supreme – a Good Education, Lots of Opportunity, and the Free to be Enterprising System. They are the three empty shells of our Confidence game. Can you find the pea? "You look like a smart fellow. Step right up and try your luck. Let me razzle-dazzle these little upside down cups around on this tray a little bit. Okay now. Where's the pea? Point to it. No, not there. Oh, ha, ha, ha. No. Keep trying."

Good Education + Hard Work = Success. Oh, yes, we all know the formula for success. Nobody knows the formula for sodium carbonhydrate, but you ask any fellow on the street the formula for success, and he'll tell you. But let's let the cat out of the bag a little. How many of you here are college graduates? Don't be ashamed. It could happen to anyone. Thank you. A scattering of you brave souls raised your hands.

I'LL BE A SOPHOMORE IN THE FALL.

Good for you, young man. Make the most of it, my friend. I'm not blaming you students, mind you. You don't know any better. Your parents are Muddled, so naturally you're going to be Muddled, too. You think that because you're at a university that a big, stuffed leather chair is being reserved just for your behind, that a place is being set aside for you with the high polloi. Oh, my, what a rude and uncouth awakening is in store for you when the sun sets on your mortarboard hat. Some of you boys are going to wake up the next morning and find that the world has a good, money-making use you can put that mortarboard to. All you'll need to go with it are a trowel and some mortar, and you'll be all set to start your first job.

Oh, yes, you think life Out There is going to be like life at the university, where a conveyor belt moves you along at a nice steady pace, year after year – Freshman – Sophomore – Junior – Senior – until almost without doing anything at all, there you are, an Upper Classman. A member of the Upper Class in only four years. Imagine what you'll be able to accomplish in a whole lifetime.

Then the graduate graduates and reality sets in. He comes out an eager Bachelor and finds out the Big Money is already married. That's when he settles down to his real-life occupation. That's when he starts Hankering. College education, that's where they get you. That's your Waterloo. You're Napoleon until you graduate, then it's the Island of Saint Helena, to hanker and hanker for the rest of your days. But you never lose hope. You still think, Some day I'm going to be Up There.

They've got you all muddled up.

We ought to stop this stranding a whole class of young people every June 5th. We shouldn't graduate anybody that doesn't meet the standards but if they do meet the standards we ought to see that they get some place to use those standards. It seems to me they've got that much coming to them, our young people do. We shouldn't take their money for four years and then leave them with nothing but a tassel and a satchel full of debt. That's just not right.

BUT WE'RE STILL IN A RECESSION.

Well, then there ought to be a money-back guarantee on the colleges we've been sending our young people to. If your daughter doesn't get the kind of job they've been filling her head with for four years, you get your money back. Satisfaction guaranteed or your money back. That's fair, isn't it? Even girdle makers are willing to give you that much. The diploma industry ought to do the same.

Yes, the Well-To-Do have those forty-carat lives, but the Muddle Class has that one carrot dangled out in front of them, talking about that Opportunity waiting Out There for everybody of Talent and Hard Work and a Good Education. Your poor children! You tell them that the sure way to get ahead is a Good Education, even though you know as well as I do that the only sure way to get ahead is to be born ahead. But you don't tell your children that because it might not reflect so well on you. So you tell them they'll find Opportunity Out There if they get a Good Education and Work Hard. They take your advice. Then, four years later, after the commencement exercise, they commence to hankering. Those poor souls step Out There with their plans and hopes and find there's nothing waiting for them but hankering.

There are a few universities where you can get a Good Education that pretty much does guarantee you some Opportunity -- Princeton and the other Envy League schools.

ENVY.

Pardon me, Sir?

ENVY. THAT'S YOUR PROBLEM. ENVY.

It was. You're right, Sir. It surely was, for a time. A very long time. But now I'm all envied out. How much can a man envy? You reach your limit and you can't do anymore. You try, but you just can't. Something just snaps inside, and the thing won't function anymore.

I know my offspring won't be going to any of those Envy League schools. And it's too bad for them, too, because when you get a diploma from one of those schools, most of the time a set of rich parents goes right along with it.

Harvard. Oh, yes, Harvard. Harvard was founded in sixteen-something to turn out ministers, and it's been turning out the high priests of our civilization ever since. Sing along with me, my friends –

SIS BOOM BAH

Harvard and Yale,
Harvard and Yale,
Oxford and Cambridge,
Rah! Rah! Rah!

Harvard and Yale,
Harvard and Yale,
Cambridge and Oxford,
Sis! Boom! Bah!

Yale and Harvard
Oxford and Yale,
Cambridge, Cambridge,
Ask you pa!

YOU SOUND LIKE A COMMIE TO ME.

A communist? Now, why should I trust the masses? If they're so smart, why aren't they rich?

GO OVER TO RUSSIA WHERE YOU BELONG.

No, folks. No, no, my friends. Let the man speak. Let him have his say. It's a free country. Let him speak his mind. But, Sir, didn't your mother ever tell you not to judge books by their covers or lovers by their looks? If I go to church on Sunday, does that make me Christian? If I don't, does that mean I'm not?

Anyway, we in America don't have separate classes the way they have in Europe. It may look as if we do, but that's an illusion. It's just that some people have a lot more money than everybody else. We do have low class neighborhoods and we have high class neighborhoods, but that's real estate, not people. If all the people in those low-class neighborhoods would just up and move, we wouldn't have any low-class neighborhoods. But they don't move. They just stay right where they are. They're stubborn, I guess. I don't know.

No, the Reds have one or two colorful ideas, but it's such a Muddled Class theory. And it wasn't poor people who came up with it. Oh, no. It took a member of the Muddled Class to come up with a theory like that. It seems to me that communism is a Muddled Class trick to get the poor to do their fighting for them. That's what it looks like in operation. Communism is the girl in the bar who comes up and tells you that the fellow in the fancy clothes over there has been saying insulting things about you. Likely as not, she's just stirring up a fight, hoping the two of you will knock each other out and leave her in peace.

I don't see that the Communists are very communistic anyway. Certainly not the Russians, anymore, not since President Reagan ordered Mr. Gorbachev to tear down that wall and put in some Wall Street. And look at the Great Wall Street of China. My Lord, today we have to borrow capital from the Chinese communists to keep our capitalism from falling into the red.

Communism? It seems like Communism is just Capitalism without the top hat. The whole thing's very muddled. You hear the Communists going on about how the Rich are bound to fall, that the whole thing is leaning over 45 degrees already, and all it'll take to topple it is one little puff. All I can say is, Don't hold your breath or refuse sexual affection until that day comes. The Communists say the Fabulous Few are doomed to failure and collapse. Well, I agree that the reign of the Fabulous Few is fading and will come to an end in time. I give them until the sun burns itself out, and then that's it!

Trialogue 4

Into the Maëlstrom
The Wrong House by Mistake
The Only Rigid Body in Nature

I attribute all of my unhappiness today to the fact that I was not breastfed. My mother was not a mammal. Those first few months didn't count. That was a tease. She teased me then plugged me into the udder of a cow. No wonder I'm the way I am. I admit it. I'm a sick man. Where is the wet nurse when you really need her?

>   BOSOM
> *If life be soul, and that soul divine,*
> *If soul be psyche, and, if psyche, breath,*
> *No nobler temple could that soul enshrine.*
> *No other lure could lure me but the lure of death.*

I wasn't always like this. It used to be that I could sit on my bed and become completely absorbed in a good book. The world would pass away, and I would become a spiritual being. But lately I can't seem to concentrate. While my eyes are reading the words, my mind is picturing a woman's upper fleshiness. Those images come uninvited. They slither in between the lines on the page, between the words, between the letters. They nest on vowels, roost on consonants.

Is this mammose obsession the doppelgänger of my infantile imagination? Am I simply being immature, emotionally flat-chested? Am I deranged? Should I have myself committed to a coëducational institution? All I know is that I can't walk a straight line in the presence of a mammacopious female. I become strangely uncoördinated. When I see a joy-breasted female in a low-cut dress, whose liquous pair threatens to overspill their banks like the rain-swollen curves of the Potomac after a storm, I fall headlong into a maëlstrom.

Why wasn't I born in France where they understand these things? Whenever I call to mind a lactiferous and willing female, something unstoppable happens, something best expressed by the Gallic term, *érection*. I'll be walking through the mall, minding my own business, when I spot a fleshy female. I try to remain unmoved but my grey matter boils to a blue purée and my body takes on an added bit of décor. I try to keep a low profile, but how can a person who's just sprouted an extra limb remain blasé? Is it just my hopeless naïveté?

I did find some relief in studying the texts of the great spiritual mystics. After a month of studying the masters of self-denial I was cured of stray thoughts almost completely. But I backslid. I am a failed mystic, a monk manqué. I try to stand on my own two feet, but biology throttles me to my knees. All I do is lay my head on the pillow and I wake up with semé sheets. Vivid dreams visit me, strange, bizarre, surréal. I once had a billiard dream in which I energetically sank a two-ball massé shot and woke up with a double hernia.

What am I supposed to do? This automatic, stimulus-response, breast-bone reaction is Nature's doing. Clearly, it is Nature's overmastering desire that I dedicate all of my energies to arriving, somehow, some day, at the ultimate destination, the delectable Hôtel Love.

. . .

Some folks are born rich, others are born wishful. You Muddled Class parents, when you're not wishing for yourselves you're wishing for your children. You're wishing for them even before they're born. The nervous father paces back and forth in the waiting room. Finally, he can't take it anymore. He drops to his knees, clasps his hands in prayer, raises his eyes to heaven, and blurts out, "O, Lord God and Master, Creator of the Universe, I don't say you have to make my child President of the United States, but, for pity's sake, at least make him a Republican."

Some folks are born with a silver spoon in their mouth, others are born with a silver spoon dangling in front of their mouth, and they spend the rest of their lives trying to get that spoon *in*. It seems so close! Their mouth waters until their tongue is waterlogged and the Niagara River is just up falls of their lower lip. Those folks I call members of the Drooling Class.

The Drooling Class is always hankering after things that are just out of reach. That's how they know they really want something – if it's just out of reach. Well, isn't it unAmerican to want what you can have? How is it going to help the economy if people are satisfied with what they've got? The whole economy is based on you hankering. Your hankering is the engine that makes the whole thing go. Many people don't understand how the Rolls Royce car can give such a quiet ride. It's very simple. It's because there's no engine under the hood. There's just a short member of the Drooling Class on a treadmill, running after a tiny Rolls Royce dangling out in front of him, just out of reach.

YOU WOULDN'T LIKE TO BE RICH, I SUPPOSE.

Oh, we all want to sit in the back seat of a Rolls. We all idolize the idle rich. We all want to get in on some of that Lazy's Fair economics. We all feel it's against human dignity for a man to do his own drudgery. We want somebody else to drive us in traffic. We don't want to mow our own lawn. We want to have servants to polish our silverware for us. That's one of the great maxims of our religion, "Lay up treasures upon earth where rust can tarnish, and then *hire* somebody to keep it shiny." That's why we have a free economy, isn't it, so some people can get rich enough to afford servants? What else is freedom for?

No man can serve two masters, but some masters can afford two servants – a Japanese gardener and a Mexican cleaning lady. Wouldn't that be heaven on earth? How about an English butler and a German chauffeur? Maybe an old Russian aristocrat to teach your young daughter the ballet, and a red man to lead your little son around on pony? An Italian cook and a French upstairs maid? How about an Italian cook and a French maid *upstairs*? Am I getting warmer? Are you? Eat your heart out. The Number One killer in the country today is heart disease. We're all eating our hearts out over the things that are hard to come by. We walk around thinking we were born below our station. It's the sickness of the age.

We look round our neighborhood and feel it's not up to our standard and we think, This can't be. I must have been switched at birth, back in the maternity ward, or the stork went to the wrong house by mistake. We see that other fellow getting everything served to him on a silver platter and we think, That lucky stiff. And we eat our hearts out. We have heart omelet for breakfast, heart casserole for lunch, and cardiac stew for dinner. We're all eaten up over our meager salary because we aren't earning enough Respect. How am I supposed to command Respect on the salary they're paying me? How am I going to strike envy in the hearts of my countrymen on these wages?

We've all got a bad case of heart disease, and you know what the New York Specialist says will cure us? Consumption. That's right. According to the New York Specialist consumption cures heart disease. That's what the Madison Avenue doctor would have us believe. And, of course, we believe him. We're all dying of attacks of the heart, and yet the Constitution says we shall be protected from unreasonable seizures. Is the United States of ADmerica unConstitutional?

If you will bear with me, folks, I'd like to recite a little something I penned for you. Here goes.

THE BALLAD OF THE MUDDLED CLASS

Oh, I feel so bad.
I just can't get it right.

I can't help myself.
I can't sleep at night.

I got the cash nexus in my solar plexus,
And it's causing me so much pain.
I got the cash nexus in my solar plexus,
It keeps eating away at my brain.

I'm so tired,
Sick and tired of that stuff,
I can't help myself.
I just can't get enough.

I got the cash nexus in my solar plexus
And it's making me go insane.
And that hurts.

. . .

My landlady said it again: "She stares into space." Yes, but there is a difference between us. I actually see space when I look into it. When she looks in the same direction she sees an empty area she'd like to fill with a new armchair from the Neiman Marcus catalog.

Meat eaters can never stare into space. Einstein mastered the mathematics of living without solid food and rendered it in his brilliant formula $E = mc^2$. We do not need solid food or solid anything. We are not matter. We are energy. E, not m. There is no such thing as matter. That hard solid stuff we used to call matter no longer exists. Only the prescientific mind can form any idea of it at all. Today materialism has become not only distasteful but completely unthinkable. There are no rigid bodies in Nature. The only rigid body in Nature is the Republican Party. The Republicans will never win election if they do not follow the recommendations I laid out in my letter to the Republican Party Chairman. Fifty-two pages, single-spaced.

Seven weeks after mailing it I received a one-sentence reply. Seventeen words. But that was to be expected. They want you to go on thinking that objects exist and that you have to own more and more of them. Don't they understand? Matter is nothing but energy in a temporarily arrested form. All acquisition is therefore the worship not of enterprise but of inertia. Life is not about objects. Life is about energy. Jesus turned into Energy and Light. He was the first atomic explosion. They would understand that if they read the Bible. But they don't read the Bible. They prefer to hide it away in the cheap hotel rooms of their minds. Are they so enamored of that undertaker God who lowers his face to ours only after we are quite dead? God is light. We are light. The Republican Party refuses to acknowledge this. We do not have to go on eating solid food. Mister Chairman, heed my letter!

Our nation was founded by men who were near gods. How far we have fallen. This country went from demigods to demagogues in three generations. The presidency itself has become a common thing. Being at least thirty-five years of age has gone from the one prerequisite to the sole qualification. All that remains of a once proud tradition is the old blindfold party game of pinning the presidency on the donkey, or the pachyderm. And what is the result? The moral power of the United States is on the wane. We are living in an era of national detumescence.

I saw that boy again this morning, the one with the beautiful, Lincolnesque face. Stand that boy and Abraham Lincoln side by side and you would have to squint and close one eye to tell them apart. They're about the same height. But really it's that face, such world-weariness, such kindness, such sadness behind the eyes. I'm thinking of the photograph of Lincoln taken a day before he was assassinated, showing his eyes already dead and a smile that might have been set by the fingers of an undertaker, that picture where the line of the cracked photographic plate cuts across the top of his head.

That boy may be cracked in the head, too. He is a strange one certainly. I like that about him.

2.

Trialogue 5

The American ZZ-ZZ Fly
A Blonde and A Banknote
Master, Eat

I don't cotton to any democracy where you're only the equal of the fellow next to you on the economic pyramid. What a man is worth is what he's worth. That's what you call Dollar Democracy. Its symbol is the pyramid.

Since it's the most important symbol in America, it's got to be on the most important piece of paper in America. What's the most important piece of paper in America? If you thought it was maybe the Declaration of Independence or the Constitution, you get another try. They put the symbol of Dollar Democracy on the dollar bill. That way we'll keep it always before our eyes.

Bring a dollar bill up out of your wallet right now and take a good look at it. Go ahead. I'll wait.

That's it. Good. Now, turn it over to the green side and you'll see the symbol of Dollar Democracy in that circle over on the left. I see some of you don't have your dollars out. Folks, if the person beside you doesn't have a dollar, share yours with him or her. Just for a minute! You'll get it back!

Sir, excuse me, Sir. The gentleman walking away through the crowd there. You don't have to share your dollar. I was just kidding. Come back, please.

I HAVE TO GET BACK TO THE OFFICE.

Oh, I sympathize entirely.

SEE YOU TOMORROW. I COME HERE EVERY DAY.

Okay, then. And bring a dollar with you next time.

I'LL SEE IF I CAN SCARE ONE UP.

Bless you, my brother. Now, those of you in the congregation who are staying to the end of the service, take a look at the green side of that all-important piece of paper in your hand. You see that pyramid I was talking about? All Americans are represented on that pyramid, somewhere or other. The ones on the top are the Fabulous Few, the One Percent. They have a separate little pyramid all to themselves Up There on top. You can see their very own symbol right in the middle of their very own pyramid. Their symbol is an Eye, because the Eyes have it.

You can see how the tip of the pyramid is floating on air in its own little Heaven on Earth, totally separate from the rest down below. That's because the tip of the pyramid doesn't have anything to do with the lower-down group. In the disUnited States of America, we don't have fifty states. We have two – the Well-To-Do and the Well-To-Don't. We like to picture ourselves as one big happy family. That's what psychiatrists call wishbone thinking. I wish we were one big happy family, but it's hard for the dinosaur to put its arm around the ant for the family portrait.

What we have in this country is right there on the dollar. We have the Fabulous Few with their own little floating crap game Up There on top. Between the Fabulous Few and all the rest of us you see there's a big empty space of hot air. That represents the politicians. It's no secret. The Elect and the Elected, Up There together. It's right there on the dollar. Why should they try to hide it from us? How could they?

Below the Elect and the Elected comes the great solid Muddled Class. And, for the picture to be complete, it has to show me and my kind also. We're included in there, too. Didn't I say all Americans are represented on that pyramid somewhere or other? Me and my kind are there, but you can't see us. We're underneath. But at least we *know* where we stand.

If you're not underneath and you're not floating Up There, and you're confused about just where you belong on that pyramid, you're a member of the Muddled Class.

D. C., WHAT ABOUT THAT OTHER CIRCLE ON THE DOLLAR, THE ONE ON THE RIGHT SIDE? DOES IT HAVE ANY SPECIAL SIGNIFICANCE, SOME SECRET, HIDDEN MEANING?

Secret meaning? No. We have no secrets here. Everything is right out front for all to see. What you see there in the circle on the right is our national bird, all green and spread-eagle, choking on a ribbon he's picked up that reads, "*E Pluribus Unum,*" Out of Many There Is One Percent.

Now let's get back to that circle with the pyramid. The Muddled Class are all tugging on their bootstraps, trying to pull themselves Up There to that separate little pyramid of the Fabulous Few. But look closely, my friends. Notice there's no ladder actually going Up There. The Haves burned that bridge behind them a long time ago. They burned their bridges behind them so you couldn't get Up There with them. Of course, they're not going to come out and say so. They're too smart for that. Their official story is, "Your eyes are not deceiving you. There is no bridge there, but we didn't burn our bridges behind us. You burned your bridges *ahead* of you." That's what their official story claims, and you know what the funny part is? You believe it. You go around thinking you could have got Up There to the *E Pluribus Unum* pyramid if only you hadn't lost your nerve, if only you hadn't taken a wrong step, if only you hadn't burned your bridges ahead of you.

But you look up and you see that little pyramid Up There on top, and it seems so close! And you think, Maybe it's not too late for me. Maybe, if I give it another try. And you keep picking dollars so you can purchase a late-model automobile and chase the hood ornament of Upward Mobility all over town. Oh, yes, this is the land of big schemes, limousines, and golden dreams that never die. You've fallen into that American Dreaminess which convinces you you were born below your station. You've been bit by the good ole American ZZ-ZZ fly. And once you're bit, brother, you stay bit. You're lost in the American Dreaminess, and there's nothing medicine or the minister can do for you. What about you? Are you living in an American Dream world?

The Muddled Class is usually dozing in its American Dreaminess but it wakes up during an economic downturn. They have different names for those things. "Correction" is one of my favorites. But I like to use the term depression. A depression is a crash course in economics for the Muddled Class. The Rich and the Poor don't get all that bothered when a depression hits. They understand the Down-Trickler has a tendency to go on the blink now and then. But to the Muddled Class it always comes as a surprise. They get very glum about it, even suicidal. Not the black man. He knows better. When the suicidal windows start opening up on the not-quite-top stories, it's not going to be a black toe you see testing the air. Neither the black men nor the Really Rich men get too disturbed when a depression hits. You have never seen a Really Rich man, just because the Down-Trickler went on the blink, open up the window of his Rolls Royce and jump out, have you?

You see, every now and then the Fabulous Few get irked at the Hankering Horde always playing the fool, pretending they belong Up There. So every once in a while the Well-To-Do stage a depression to shake the hangers-on off. In the worst of times the economic pyramid starts to sink until only the tip can keep its head above water. You Muddled Class fellows need to be reminded once in a while which side of the waterline you really belong on. So the order goes out to turn the Down-Trickler off, just like that. Then the totem pole you thought you were shimmying up turns into a grease pole between your legs and, "Look out below!"

Yet in the picture on the dollar that pyramid looks so solid, doesn't it? Did you ever imagine it would fall so suddenly? And on *your* head? But remember your Bible. The good Lord said it: "The Rich and the Poor shall always be with you, but the Muddled Class can disappear overnight." You didn't know that. You thought money in the bank was like money in the bank.

SOUR GRAPES.

Pardon me, Sir?

I SAID SOUR GRAPES.

Sir, with me it's a case of no grapes. I'd be willing to accept sour grapes. Even sour raisins would taste good to me. When you're underneath the economic pyramid, the pickin's are *slim*.

Actually, I'm not put out by the way things have gone down. I don't worry myself too much about it. The black man is used to depressed times. He's been trained to them. The black man is king of conspicuous-by-its-absence consumption. But the black man at least knows his altitude on the pyramid. He knows what latitude he's been allowed. He knows he's a member of the Well-To-Don't. But what about you? Can you pick out your particular stone on that pyramid, the one with your name on it? And I don't mean where you hope you'll end up when things *pick* up. I mean right now.

Depressed times can't confuse me or hurt me and my kind a great deal. You can't get much lower on that pyramid than underneath it. It's not the best real estate in the world, but at least we know where we are. Our minds are not confused, and that's important. The Lord is my Shepherd. Though I may be as broke as the Tenth Commandment, I shall not want.

I see that many of you still have those dollar bills in your hands. They would fit very nicely in this hat I'm now passing among you. Thank you, brother and sisters. Thank you. Thank you. Thank you. Thank you. God bless you.

. . .

I can't believe my good luck! Thank you, God. Thank you, God. Thank you, God. That brunette in the movie-star sunglasses was there again this morning. She was carrying a book, and not just any book but a copy of Edgar Allan Poe's *The Philosophy of Furniture*. For the last year and a half I've been carrying around a copy of *The Philosophy of Furniture* believing that one day I'd recognize Miss Right because she'd be carrying the same book!

That day has come sooner than I expected. I'm not sure I'm ready for it. What if she had seen me the other day with the book and decided she wanted to read it? Or it may just be a coincidence. I didn't go ahead and approach her this morning because the way I had it set up Miss Right was supposed to come up to me and say, "Excuse me, young man, is that a copy of Edgar Allan Poe's *The Philosophy of Furniture* in your pocket or are you just glad to see me?" Didn't happen.

She's probably just a gold-digging female after the money I expect to make after I graduate. With men money is the means and women are the end. With women it's the other way around. A man wants one thing, but a woman wants many, many things. That's why blondes prefer gentlemen. That's why you often see a most stultifyingly beauteous woman walking down the street with a study in contrast. Charm and sincerity seem to count for little with them. I've discovered that a reasonably non-repulsive appearance and a sound character have little power to melt that block of ice. But money works like a blowtorch.

Don't expect to make it with a ball-raising female unless you've got a bankroll as round and green as the waves at Maui. It's what bulges in the back of a man's pants that stimulates them. You've got to approach them backwards.

HUMAN
If she would but call,
Upon her neck I'd fall,
Just like a warming shawl.
I'm human.

At the faintest beck
I'd give her cheek a peck.
What do you expect?
I'm human.

Why won't she comply?
Why is she with that guy?
Because she wants the sky.
She's human.

Who ever heard of a girl getting ready for a date by doing something sensible, like brushing up on the anatomy and physiology of the male reproductive system? Instead she spends her time trying to make herself look like a woman of leisure, a woman who appreciates luxury. She senses the connection between a blonde and banknote.

A blonde lives across the street from me. Yesterday I saw her at the apex of her semicircular driveway washing the pink sports car her boyfriend bought her. She spent forty-five minutes wetting, soaping, rubbing and rinsing, getting that car slick and shiny. Why did she lavish forty-five minutes of love on a piece of brute machinery when I – a living, heavily breathing human being – was available right across the street? I'll tell you why – because that car can take her where she wants to go in style, and I can't. If I had big bucks, you could bet your life she'd be knocking on my door. I would open it and there she'd be, swiveling within the pink circle of her patent leather belt.

My father drives a Rolls. But it's leased. He puts up a good front but he doesn't have enough money for me to really lower my standard of living. I'm going to be so wealthy some day I'm going to have a chauffeur drive me around town in an automobile transport truck stacked with Bentleys and Ferraris, with their noses in the air.

. . .

I would have pleaded with Einstein not to leave Germany. Stay in Germany and be martyred. I would have said: Our era has need of a saint. If you go to America your work of '05 will be distorted and applied to developing the most dastardly device ever foisted upon mankind. You will go down in history as the father of – television. "I am not a saint. I am a scientist," he would have said. But if you go to America you will cease to be a scientist. You will never have another idea. They will see to it. They will send you to a university, where people go to stop having ideas. Cadavers were once used in American universities to teach anatomy. Now they're propped up to teach upper division seminars in moral philosophy. Don't leave Germany! What is worse, Hitler or a life without ideas? The Germans will burn your books, yes. If you go to America they will not burn your books but they will never open them. They will let them collect dust on the shelf. But they will put your picture everywhere.

Professor Einstein, they are blaming you for the atomic bomb. And they have the audacity to claim dropping it saved lives.

America eggs its intellectuals then wonders why it has no thinkers of the first rank. America is a chicken without a head, looking for where it mislaid its glasses. I have been laughed at. As a baby my first word was "rhubarb." They all laughed. I could have said "Mama" or "Papa" but I would have felt silly. I was already using the higher centers of my brain. Wasn't Gauss correcting his father's calculations at three years old? Before I was seven I had taught myself to read Latin. I wanted to read Hobbes in the original.

Not one philosophical journal will publish my articles. They say they are not in proper form. Are Leonardo da Vinci's journals in proper form? Leonardo has been dead for five hundred years, and they're still calling his paintings unfinished.

I am working on a formulation that cannot be refuted. That horde of spoil-paper editors! Especially a certain professor, editor of a certain journal of symbolic logic, who rejected my repeated submittals but showed a warm interest in my work the minute I collapsed from exhaustion in the corridor outside his office. I had hitchhiked in the rain all the way from Virginia. I'd walked the final six miles, with a broken heel in my hand. But I made it to his door. He was working late. There was no one else in the building. When I collapsed he picked me up, carried me into his office, and set me down on a shabby leather couch.

I handed him my manuscript kept dry in a plastic bag. He took a long time reading it, so I granted his request. I felt I owed it to him. It was a sweaty, philosophical performance, a carefully worked syllogism in logical form, with a major premise and a minor premise. Everything, in fact, but a conclusion.

He permitted me to sleep on that cracked leather couch which not only reeked of pipe tobacco but felt as if it were stuffed with Prince Albert. He insisted I be out of there before dawn. And I was. But his promise was never kept. A year passed. My article never appeared in his journal. A little later my manuscript arrived in the mail, coffee-stained, with pipe ash between the pages. On the last page he had written a note saying nothing about that night but ending with, "You have a brilliant future if only you would handle a few details better." He made suggestions that proved he had understood absolutely nothing.

American men prefer a beautiful to an intelligent woman. They run headlong into the arms of beauty, no matter that beauty gives nothing, takes all, then destroys itself. Men prefer blondes because it is assumed that blond hair about the genito-anal region promises freedom from defecation and, therefore, from the disgusting habit of thought. That is why the blonde is expected to be dumb.

My landlady is waiting to see if I find a publisher for my book. She is curious about what the critics will say. She wants to see if it will sell! She's just like the rest of them, waiting to find out from the others. They wouldn't let Rudolph join in any reindeer games because his nose was too shiny. But as soon as Santa chose him to guide the sleigh that foggy night, how all the reindeer loved him. Vermin! They used to laugh and call him names, then all of a sudden all the reindeer loved him. You have to go down in his-to-ry. Idiots!

It's for my landlady's sake that I don't talk to her. I'm terrified that if I spoke my mind and fired a volley of hard sentences at her, the periods would smash into her like buckshot. "A friend of mine's son died over the weekend. He completed law school." Those are her words. No wonder both her husbands left her.

Even as an infant I refused solid food. Even then the act of chewing filled me with revulsion -- the tongue, sodden with salivation, shoving morsels of solid food down the big hole like a sweaty stevedore. Solid food cannot produce ideas, just that vile little monster in the bowels, taking only the worst, the lifeless, the useless, the exhausted, encrusting itself time over time, embolding itself in size, dimension, and arrogance. A fat ferret, round the serpentine sewers of the body it slithers slow as justice, taking on weight. In the end, immobile, sedentary, petulant, demanding, it drags you to a field of green flies and beckons you to give it air. Afterwards, you hobble away as if from some unspeakable crime or horrifying accident. It is too absurd. I will have none of it.

A few days ago a man who was holding *The Wall Street Journal* exposed himself to me on the bus while I was reading Alexander Hamilton's *A Full Vindication of the Measures of the Congress from the Calumnies of Their Enemies*. I exited the bus. The man exited the bus. He walked behind me with that newspaper open before him. I wheeled around shouting, "Why are you following me!"

Completely unabashed he said, "Because you have the most beautiful ass I've ever seen." I snatched his newspaper and heaved it billowing into the air. He yanked his fly up on the run, frantically waving with his other hand to hail a taxi, as if it were the last cab out of Sodom.

Jesus would no more eat meat than sell Bibles door to door. His disciples prayed him, saying, "Master, eat." But he said unto them, "I have meat to eat that ye know not of." The disciples did not understand. They thought he was hoarding food. We don't need solid food. With rational planning the human race can eliminate feces in two generations.

Trialogue 6

What Is She Thinking About Right Now?
A Moderately Large Idaho Potato
Aunt Bertha's Toes

I brought my dog-eared copy of Poe's *The Philosophy of Furniture* every day this week, but Miss Right was nowhere to be found. Anyway, her hair color was wrong. And what are the odds that beneath the book's dust jacket she, too, would be carrying a copy of Krafft-Ebing's *Psychopathia Sexualis*?

I'm suffering from lower front pain. Why won't my health insurance honor my claim? I believe I have correctly diagnosed my condition – an uncontrollable and insatiable sexual desire in the male. The doctor I spoke with on the phone said it is considered a preexisting condition, having existed since the beginning of time. It's normal, for the male, but if a female suffers from a corresponding condition, it's considered an illness. I can't believe this world.

Doc, I'm in a city-full of pain, a satyr in the city, feeling the urge to tup someone right now. Why doesn't the Surgeon General do something? I'm in a constant state of Must: a condition of dangerous frenzy, connected with sexual excitement, said of male elephants. Why not said of female elephants, too? In my more than nineteen years I have never met a female in Must. All the females I meet are in Maybe.

The problem with females is that they are not thinking about sex all the time. What *do* they think about? How do females use their excess consciousness? I don't know. Maybe they don't suffer from excess consciousness the way males do. Maybe females percolate only the exact amount of consciousness necessary for the task at hand.

Take that blonde in the two-piece swimsuit the same color red you see when you close your eyes and look up into the sun. There she floats in the donut hole of a black inner tube -- brushing her hair. What is she thinking about right now, I wonder? The horrible truth is I know the answer: She's thinking about brushing her hair. If I were to dogpaddle over there and call out, "What are you thinking about right now?" chances are she'd shout back, "I'm brushing my hair."

I'd yell out, "I can see you're brushing your hair, but what are you thinking about *while* you're brushing your hair?"

"Thinking about?"

"Yes, thinking about."

She'd take a moment, then answer, "I'm thinking about getting the tangles out." And she would be in dead earnest. Where did estrus go? How could our ancestors let something that useful slip through their hairy fingers? Yes, well, we moderns needn't pine over lost instincts; we have a big advantage over our forest fathers. We can pass laws. I'll start a petition to bring estrus back. Think I could count on the support of the League of Women Voters?

Can't people see that the animals have it better? You don't see chimpanzees escorting their mates to dinner and a movie before getting down to basics. They dispense with the economic foreplay. Monkeys don't write sonnets or bring bouquets of flowers. They don't need to. The female chimpanzee *presents* herself, and the male presents himself. It's that simple. When the male is in Must, the female is in Certainly. To make things even simpler, the female in heat gives the male chimp a very clear go-ahead sign. She turns her backside to him and her not-at-all-private parts commence to swell up and turn bright pink. Now, doesn't that take all the guesswork out of it?

The chimpanzee knows just what he needs to know, but *homo non-sapiens* is always in the dark. We human males never get such useful help in knowing what it is the prime business of our lives to know: Is she feeling itchy or bitchy. If we were still on all-fours we could look for coming shades of pink but, standing erect, we are confused.

Primal example: this afternoon I thought I spied Miss Right walking on the Mall near the Smithsonian. I was coming out of the Institution when I saw, way up ahead through the bobbing heads of the tourist throng, a brunette. Now and then I could see she was carrying something that might have been that special book. By weaving through the crowd I tried to get close enough to make a positive identification, but she kept moving at a good clip. Now and then she looked back without slowing her pace. Was she egging me on or trying to lose me? I was finally gaining some ground when I collided at full speed with a Japanese tour guide walking slowly backwards. We both went sprawling, and three more camera-totting tourists fell like dominos.

By the time I had picked myself up and hurriedly helped the visitors to their feet, the brunette had vanished. Still, I pressed on. Just before turning for home I thought I saw her walking up the steps to the Library of Congress. Was she trying to tell me something by leading me to the library of -- congress? Is that slightly older woman trying to seduce me?

. . .

My letter to the Republican Party Chairman made everything plain. I stand with John Randolph, one of our greatest statesmen, who stood upon the floor of Congress and declared he loved Liberty but hated equality. Liberty is the great thing. The natural aristocracy of this country must rule, without apology. The people cannot be trusted with important matters of state. The Founding Fathers understood this. Equality for all was never the intention. Universal suffrage was far from their minds. One man, one vote – two insignifications. The President must act for the good of all.

Of, By and For The People? Have you ever stood downwind of democracy? Not equality but nobility should be the aim. What kind of nobility may we expect of a political system that compels its finest souls to submit to the judgment of 50% plus my landlady? The *aristoi* are the only true aristocracy.

Should the opportunity ever fall to the People's lot to decide any matter of supreme importance, I am sure they could be counted on to act with all the sober judgment of a mob in an earthquake. There can be little doubt that in matters of justice, in matters of policy, in matters of principle, theology, philosophy or just plain good sense, the common man presents to an impartial observer a mind that can grasp nothing of the utmost importance, a mind unencumbered by thought, a riot of ignorance, not the ignorance of Plato's Cave but of the cave dwellers of old, a wild conflagration of ignorance, an ignorance luxuriant, prolific, a quadrupedal, cloven-hoofed, rapacious, insatiable ignorance devouring everything in its path, an ignorance that prostrates all patience, all wisdom, all compassion, and all this within the compass of a narrow-mindedness so severe there is ample room in that cranium on both sides of the brain for a moderately large Idaho potato.

Behold the great and sovereign American vote casters. Put them behind the chintz curtain of a voting booth, and they are as giddily beside themselves as Siamese twins in a funhouse mirror. Solon of the voting lever, Nebuchadnezzar of the newscast, Hammurabi of the Headline. Here is the slob who has the gall to peak out over the rim of his beer belly to lower his sports section and declare, *"L'état c'est moi!"*

. . .

Have you read the Emancipation Proclamation lately? Do you know what it says? It says that the North has decided to free all the slaves – in the southern states! The South should have returned the favor and freed all the slaves in the North where they did not exist. That would have made it unanimous. Then the slaves would have been free in every state except those they happened to be in.

Still, I love the Emancipation Proclamation. I love all our great American documents. The United States of America is the greatest country, on paper, the world has ever known.

PREACH, BROTHER.

Bless you, Sister.

America loves declaring the black man free and equal, on paper. America loves it so much she does it all over again every hundred years or so. Thomas Jefferson created all of us equal, on paper, back in July of 1776. That was a good thing. Abe Lincoln Proclaimed us Emancipated, on paper, In 1862. About a century later, In the 1960s, President Lyndon Johnson declared us equal again. Pretty soon, watch out, another hundred years will roll by, and it'll again be time for our routine freeing and equalizing, on paper.

The out-of-the-bag truth is that in the United States of America all men are about as equal as Aunt Bertha's toes. Now, I don't mind so much that Aunt Bertha's toes are not equal. What I do mind, though, is that Aunt Bertha keeps saying they are.

EQUAL IN THE EYES OF THE LAW.

Yes, Sir, but that depends on how much law

you can afford. Equality and Justice for all? Seems like the French think otherwise. That's why they put up only one statue out in New York harbor, the statue of Liberty. Did you ever notice that Miss Liberty is alone out there without her two republican sisters? What do you think happened to the other two ladies, Fraternity and Equality? The French are suggesting the sister in the harbor fed the other two to the sharks. Giving us only one of the three sisters seems like France's idea of a little joke on us.

WE DON'T CARE MUCH WHAT FRANCE THINKS ABOUT US.

That's right. We don't much care what the rest of the world thinks about us. We *know* we Americans are all free and equal, and that's it. When you know something you know it, and there's no use asking damn fool questions about it. It's a Mythfact, and you don't question it.

There is no discrimination is this country. We don't have discrimination. We just have exclusive neighborhoods, exclusive clubs, exclusive restaurants, and so on, down the line. You know what "exclusive" means, don't you? It doesn't mean "of very high quality." It means that most fellows are being excluded. It means, "Rest assured, Sir, we keep the riffraff out." Which, in case you didn't happen to read the small print, means you. Not only you but most of the Presidents of the United States, too. In the really exclusive clubs, nine out of ten of our Presidents wouldn't be allowed to come in out of the rain to use the phone without a signed letter from three bona fide members.

Lack of Equality? We don't have any of that. We're all equal as People, but we do have different Groups. First there is the Inheriting Group. They have a residence in Europe. Then we have the Prosperous Group. They go to Europe once a year. Then there's the Nest Eggers. They take a trip to Europe after they retire. Finally, we have the Also-Ran Group. They have ancestors that once lived in Europe all year round.

We don't have much poverty in this country, either. What little poverty we do have is not the bad kind they have in Europe. In Europe they have the bad kind that people get stuck in and can't get out of. That's not the kind we have in this country. The kind we have here is the kind you don't have to be in at all if you really don't want to.

It's one of our great American Mythfacts that if you really want to be Rich with all your heart, you will be. If you only middlingly want to be Rich, you'll be middlingly Rich. If you don't no-how want to be Rich, you'll be that. You'll be poor, but the sting is taken right out of the thing because it's something you've chosen. What do you think this is -- Europe?

THERE'S A PLANE LEAVING EVERY HOUR.

I can't leave yet. I'm waiting for my Ship to come in. It'll be here any minute. No, I can't leave just yet.

But, you know, no matter what we're talking about, it always seems to come back to *E Pluribus Unum*, out of many there is One Percent. Tell me something. Is that Equality and Democracy as you understand it in your mind? Our great-grandfathers fought the Great War, way back when, to make the world safe for Democracy. Democracy, we made the world safe for you. You can come out now. The coast is clear. Yoo-hoo?

The bald truth is that calling ourselves a Democracy seems a little like sporting a ten dollar toupee. No one is fooled, but vanity is saved.

Trialogue 7

Hail, Realdo Colombo
Where's My White Rabbit?
Rule, Britannia!

Goddess, thy name is Woman. Aphrodite, Gaia, Hera, Frigg. It's no surprise the words that come most naturally to the lips of a male on seeing a lightning-boltingly beautiful female are, "Oh, my God, my God." All right, if not God, then God's finest handiwork and the most convincing proof of God's existence. I am a firm believer in the argument from design. Something that good does not come about by accident. There are no atheists in bed.

I am a devotee of the female sex, though my devotion is based wholly on faith. I've never had the pleasure of seeing the real thing up close. I feel sorry for any young man looking for accurate information in anatomy books. You call those illustrations? What do they show you – a cross section. Why a cross section of that subject only? When they want to illustrate the presidents of the United States, do they show them to you in cross section? No, they don't. What am I supposed to do with a cross section of that all-important subject? I can't make three-dimensional sense of it. My visual-spatial acuity is not that good.

The only thing I learned from consulting anatomy books is that an anatomist named Realdo Colombo discovered the clitoris in 1559. You may think that a rather late date to have discovered the clitoris, but I'm still looking for it.

. . .

YOU'RE GOING TO BURN IN HELL!
Sir, I have burned in hell. How do you think I got this color? Now I got him laughing. Now what was it I was about to say? Oh, yes. I remember now. I was about to say our educational system is the best in the world, bar none. And the place where all our educating originates is named after the street where it is carried out -- Madison Avenue, also known as Pavlov Ave. Does that ring a bell?

All of us are created equal in the eyes of Madison Avenue. Every American, regardless of flatnessity of nose, skin pigmentation, or edition of the Bible, is fully educated, whether he likes it or not. We all get our B.A. in Being Advertised.

A billion dollars a year goes into our B.A. degree. We're really getting the first-class treatment. Oh, yes, every mother's son in ADmerica is drilled over and over again on the three R's – Aren't you going to buy anything? Aren't you going to buy anything else? Aren't you going to buy anything *else*?

Since you're eating your heart out hankering to be Up There, Pavlov Ave supplies you with pictures of you Up There with a beautiful media pinup. You close your eyes and pucker up but when you open your eyes you find you're embracing not a female but a new automobile tire, and there's a little tag on it, and the tag says, SOLD. Did you ever try to get satisfaction from an automobile tire? But it's too late. You took the bait. The ADmerican baitsman, the White Protestant Angler Saxon of Madison Avenue, is a fisher of men, and the Hankering Horde is his favorite fry. He's got a shiny, fool's-gold hook with your name on it.

He's baited his hook with gorgeous red-headed herrings. They're everywhere you look, the glittering females, bait for the unwary male swimming in a watery ADmerican Daydream. He knows you only feel confident when you can picture yourself Up There with one of those redheaded herrings and he plays on that. It's the biggest confidence game in the country, and you're game for it.

It's the same trick duck hunters use. They know the way to attract ducks is to set out a pretty decoy where all the drakes can see it. As the drakes start coming around, duck hunters pick them off one by one. You're a drake and you crave a duck. They know that. So they put an attractive decoy out there to catch your eye. You go for it, while they go for your wallet.

But that's chickenfeed compared to a much grander game. The big money is in getting all the males to compete for the female that's hard to get, like the oh-so-desirable white rabbit in the dog races. That dreamy white rabbit exists only in the heated imaginations of the salivating dogs. But once those cages spring open and that fake white rabbit speeds away up ahead, it's off to the races!

And there you go, joining the pack and straining to be the first to get to that attractive white rabbit just out of reach. "Come on legs, carry me to her," paws pounding dirt, tongue dangling, running, running, running, panting, panting, panting, "she's lovely, so lovely, let all those other dogs eat their hearts out, she's going to be mine, mine, mine, I'm gaining on her, I'm gaining, gaining, closing in, there's her tail and there's the bell! I won! I won! Oh, thank you, God. I won. She's mine. She's.... Hey, where'd she go? Hey! Whatta ya mean, 'Back to the kennel?'

Where's my white rabbit? I raced and I won. Hey, wait a minute. Hey!"

You trot back to the kennel thinking, "What happened? I raced my heart out and I won. There must have been some technicality of some kind." And your Trainer eggs you on to believe you must have missed some technicality of some kind, something you did wrong. Yes, because your Trainer is in cahoots. Well, didn't you go to school? And didn't they train you for the track? Yes, they did. School is where you get your dog obedience training, where they prepare you for Pavlov Ave. They make you just bright enough to read the ads but not smart enough to see through them. It's when you get out of school that your real education begins. Then they can fill your empty head with good ole ADmerican Mythfacts. Then you can start your career as just another member of the Hankering Horde – a good, dog-obedient, Muddled Class Ameri-canine male. Then you can start courting success and the white rabbit, dreaming of the time when you can go before the Parson.

In the United States of ADmerica the Business Man is the only Parson. The Business Man sets the rules of courtship. It was very unBusinesslike the way Nature had left the thing, where there was a girl for every boy, and all they had to do was get together. No good! That's unBusinesslike. Money has to change hands. So the Parson took over and the Parson says, Good

Ameri-canine males want white rabbits that are hard to come by, so they have to race and fetch and pick dollars. Then they can marry, take out a mortgage, and settle down to making their banker very happy. It works like this: Boy meets Girl. Boy takes Girl to movies. Boy meets Girl's parents. Parents go upstairs. Boy sits down on couch with Girl. Boy gets down on one knee and pops the question, "I love you. Let's get mortgaged."

The mortgage, you understand, is the most important part. We're talking about marriage here, and the Business Man is the only Parson. Oh, yes, the marriage can break up, but the mortgage goes on forever. You can go to the judge and ask him to sunder the little pact between you and her. You got married, but somehow it didn't turn out the way you thought it would. "She seems like a white rabbit, but there's something human about her. That's it! She's a human being! Your honor, I object. Breach of promise! I thought she was a wooden white rabbit, and all she turns out to be is just another human being." You thought you were getting a white rabbit and all you got was mortgaged.

But you can't go back to the banker and say, "The thrill is gone. I want out." No, no, my friend. You went before the Parson, and that's it. You can cry all the way to the bank, but it won't do you a bit of good. Love may die, but the mortgage lives on and on.

What's wrong with you? Didn't you buy anything expensive today? Don't you own a house, a wife and two kids? Can't you command Respect? Isn't your sex life satisfactory? Doesn't your mortgage partner understand you?

. . .

As I made plain in my letter to the Chairman of the Republican National Committee, the gravest tragedy of the modern era in America is not the curse of war but the People's want of the warrior spirit. The very instincts of the lower orders are against the masterful. We must wage war to continue to be a great and powerful force in the world, so wars there shall be. A nation that has lost the will to conquer has forfeited its place in history. A just war? A just war is one you have just won. No nation that resorts to the concept "just war" will ever be capable of monumental architecture. Hitler's plans for Berlin as a great world capital never felt steel and concrete because even he had to justify every move to his people as a defense of the fatherland.

Look at the architectural fossil they call Washington, D.C. This is not the capital of the *Novus* Ordo Seclorum. This is an archaeological dig.

Renaissance copies, Roman copies, Greek copies, and a copy of a thyroidal Egyptian obelisk as the pinnacle of bad taste. The Egyptians knew something about war, architecture, and the warrior spirit. So did the Greeks, the Romans and the Roman Catholic Church.

The martial spirit is an aristocratic possession. Its anthem is "Rule, Britannia! Britannia rules the waves!" We deserted the aristocratic spirit and, look, we have gone from "Rule, Britannia!" to "Oh, say. Can you see if our flag is still there?" Pathetic. We have made a national anthem out of a piece of verse whose only claim to mercy is that it was composed under duress of battle. And that so-called music! Don't get me started. You know, of course, why people place a hand over their heart while singing our national anthem? They're terrified that while straining to reach those god-awful notes they'll go into cardiac arrest.

"Rule, America!" That must be our motto. We must be proud to go to war, must allow an elite class of warrior kings to lead us. Nobility. Courage. The Will to Conquer. They are our right. They are our duty. We don't have to be liked. We never liked Ike. It was to our shame that Eisenhower was selected Allied Commander over Patton. Why Eisenhower? Because of his hickocratic demeanor, so unwarlike, so uncommanding that even as world victor we did not feel in awe of the man. We simply liked him. Did anyone like George Washington? Or William Tecumseh Sherman?

Enough of these defensive wars of conquest. Why so timid? Why so shy? Why not a nation of conquerors? Abel died childless. Let us make the most of it. America is the most powerful nation in the history of the world, but we are not allowed to feel it. The unaristocratic man is uncomfortable in the role of conqueror, so we must remain the milquetoast Romans of the twenty-first century.

We see ourselves as nice. But where do you think Adolf Hitler learned what he knew? His favorite boyhood game was cowboys and Native Americans. Four score and seven years before the dawn of the Third Reich, we had already Manifested our Destiny. We had had our Lebensraum U.S.A. Why so shy?

Alaska and Hawaii? Alaska and Hawaii are not colonies. No matter that a portion of the United States lies as far from Washington, D. C., as, say, Algeria. Alaska and Hawaii are both part of the United States proper. Is it our fault that the Lord placed them where they are? Our cartographers have righted the Lord's error by situating them a short swim from our Pacific coast. Visually and mentally God's error has been corrected.

Ask my landlady. She will tell you the American people are not warlike. The American people are nice. We have no territorial ambitions. Honest Injun.

Trialogue 8

Glittering Indifference
Find a Nice Man
King Me!

I know in my mind that Beauty is in the eye of the beholder, that Beauty lives only in the rods and Coney Island of my cornea. I know covetously beautiful females are a mirage, an urban mirage for an urban thirst. I know that. I know that salivant females exist only in the lonely cavity of my skull. The first tragedy of my life is that the women of my fantasies don't really exist. The second is that they don't take to me. If Beautiful Females wanted -- no -- needed me, I could enjoy life. But they don't. They shun me. At a wedding party in June I was ruthlessly gang-shunned by fifty-seven women, including the bride.

When I move toward a ravishing female, she moves away. I get within a certain distance and she flutters off, muttering to herself. It's like trying to walk up to a pigeon. You might only want to stroke it or offer it something nice, but it won't let you. Why do touch-worthy females flutter away? If I could only get abreast of one for just fifteen minutes. Is that too much to ask?

The beauteous ones all seem so self-sufficient, the picture of glittering indifference, boredom chloroformed. I'm in a world of pain and they're as unmoved as a trained physician. All I've ever gotten when I've made goo-goo eyes at a gorgeous female is a withering, saltpetrous look.

Sometimes they insult me. More than one has told me to my face that I'm the kind of guy who would make a good husband. That's the kiss of death! Girls want to be married but not to a guy who would make a good husband. Would someone please explain that to me?

I know what's going to happen some day. I'm going to find a girl who'll agree to marry me. We'll pause for a white ceremony in a steepled chapel then drag tin all the way to Niagara, arriving just in time to watch the sun sink into the hills like a shiny penny in a child's piggy bank. That night, in a cottage mist-kissed by the Falls, my new bride will rest her head upon a pink satin pillow. I roll toward her and begin playing a little bit of night music on her well-freckled clavicle. Suddenly, up she sits with a mortified look on her face and says, "I never thought of you that way."

Will I ever find a gorgeous female willing to apply tanning cream to those easy to reach places? Look at that one in the white sundress sitting on the grass with her back against the tree, her bare feet pulled in, and her inner thighs pressed together like Vermont and New Hampshire. All I want to do is put a few inches between them. If I went up and told her what was on my mind, she would have me arrested for attempted attempt to attempt attempted sex. Why can't there be less tension between us and more friction?

There she goes nudging her strap over the falls of her shoulder. Doesn't she know what that does to me, and where? Why do I always get that look of spermicidal indifference? Was it something I thought? I could walk up to her and attempt frottage -- rubbing against the clothing of another to achieve sexual gratification. That's not much but, from what I gather, it's more than what some married men are getting.

. . .

Men know Nature prefers us. Look how Nature guards the female reproductive organ deep within the safety of our bodies. Meanwhile, the male appurtenance dangles outside, where it is subject to terrifying dangers, not the least of which is -- comparison.

Despite what males claim, the penis was fashioned not as a club to subdue uppity females but as a prostrate suppliant to venture in reverence within the sacred temple of our bodies, there, perhaps, to leave a trembling offering and, humbled, ever so slowly to withdraw.

Women are Life's creators! Men envy our life-giving role. Well, it is not as if men produce nothing at all. They have their thimbleful. But what is that beside our seven pounds, six ounces?

All the arrogant male myths about woman having been created to please the male demonstrate nothing more than sourly grappling with their secondary reproductive status. We may enjoy the game of trying to guess which came first, the chicken or the egg, but one thing's for sure: the rooster was third. For this they hate us. In his jealousy and rage at woman's life-giving role, the male devised the means to do away with the female. Finding to his chagrin that he could not dispense with her entirely, he stripped her of everything but the one essential, her womb. Thus, in a sterile lab jar he is pleased to call a home, each husband preserves a personless uterus in the acrid formaldehyde of marriage.

My landlady says I should settle down and get married. "A beautiful girl like you. Why don't you find a nice man and settle down in a nice house in the suburbs? Any man would be proud to have such a beautiful wife like you." I will not submit. Why? To what end? To be a trophy in a trophy case, gathering dust? No, thank you. I refuse to waste my days amidst the pots and pandemonium of a housewife's lot. I believe I can do more with my intelligence than pair socks.

"But don't you want to have a child of your own?" Yes, but not under those conditions. Not in times like these. Any couple that would bring children into the world today does not deserve to have them. There is only one condition under which it is justifiable to bring a child into the world: if one has the unshakable will to make that child the instrument of world historical transformation.

There is only one honorable way for a woman to have a child today and that is to will it into existence utilizing the mathematics involved. The male is not only ignorant of the mathematics of reproduction, he is blithely unconcerned with the biology involved. Sex for the male is totally unrelated to reproduction. The male does not marry to beget and nurture children. He is reluctant to sire anything, even pleasure. Sex for him is just something to do when he is not actually counting money.

Men only marry because they cannot commit adultery otherwise. Oh, the silly sins of the suburbs. The male doesn't actually covet his neighbor's wife, not earnestly, not with passion. He just goes through the motions. Such desultory adultery. We do not bother, as in Old Testament times, to throw a man to his death for sleeping with the wife of his contiguous property owner, because adultery has come to be so unlustful. There is no longer anything genuinely biblical about it. It's just weekend lust, obligatory and routine, like mowing the lawn. Back and forth, back and forth. "Boy a nice cold beer would sure go good right now."

Silly adulterous satyrs sneaking goatishly in, and sheepishly out. What a disappointment when, following a night of forbidden pleasure with a woman so much more striking than his own wet flint of a wife, he discovers that in the dark of night he had mistaken his own bedroom window for that of his neighbor. Horrors! He had climbed into bed with his own wife – and enjoyed it! How will he explain this to the boys at the Club? How will he explain it to himself?

I've had it with moonlight and flowers. I dropped the dimple act a long time ago. No more romance for this gal. I will never again let some smooth-talking male fill me full of liquid lies. They all want just two things: the first -- and no responsibility. Yesterday, I was waiting for the bus, reading Kant's *Prolegomena*, when wet splotches began appearing on the page. It was starting to snow. I walked through the nearest doorway, sat down, and bent over my book. The stool to my right was yanked back. A brute in a beard plopped himself down beside me and banged his beer mug down as if it were a bowling trophy. I kept my eyes on the page. I hoped the beard would have the decency to just go away.

The beard said, "Are you meeting someone, Miss?"

I looked up perfunctorily then went back to the page to search for the thought I had been working on. I finally rejoined minds with Kant and was settling back comfortably aboard the train of thought that now once more began slowly pulling away from the station, when the beard asked, "Are you alone?" Back to the station to slowly build up steam, then, "A beautiful girl like yourself ought to have some male companionship." I did not answer. He said, "I guess you have a boyfriend."

"No," I said. "I'm between disappointments at the moment." I was thinking of my last mistake. The less said about him would be an exaggeration. He thought he was God's Indian-gift to women. If I had any feeling left for him at all, I would despise him. I am grateful to that man for one thing. From him I learned that love supplies us with life's two most sublime experiences: falling in and getting the hell out.

The stench of beer was tickling my nose with the feather of nausea.

The beard said, "What are you reading?"

"Immanuel Kant's *Prolegomena to Any Future Metaphysics*," I answered.

"Metaphysics, huh?"

"Yes."

"I'll tell you what. Why don't you bring your

dainty little hand this direction, and I'll show you all the metaphysics you'll ever need to know."

That's when he got a mug full of beer in his lap. I pushed past and out the door in time to jump on to the bus -- with his drunken buddies laughing in the growing distance.

A while back I met a man I liked. I was waiting for the bus near a construction site. On the other side of the chain link fence a construction worker was sitting on his hardhat, eating his lunch out of an open lunch pail. He was lean. There was something about him I liked. I rested my fingers in the little rhombi of the fence. He said hello. I don't know why but I made up a story about not having a place to sleep that night. He thought a minute then said I was welcome to stay at his place. He had to get back to work. I sat in his pick-up and read Edgar Allan Poe's *The Philosophy of Furniture* until his quitting time. We didn't speak all the way to his house. There was dinner. Then his wife fixed a place for me on the couch. The baby in their bedroom cried a great deal that night. Once during the night I saw the man holding his little baby in his arms, whispering to it, walking it around. I slipped into my clothes in the dark and, with my Poe under my arm and my shoes in my hand, let myself out.

. . .

There may be something waiting for our children Out There, but I wouldn't always call it Opportunity. The door marked Going Down is the only thing always open to them.

THINGS WILL PICK UP.

I know. I know. Prosperity is just around the corner. But most of our children, even in good times, don't find that Big Time Opportunity we hear so much about over the loudspeakers. One guy in ten million gets lucky, and the newspapers say, "See." The fluke is touted as the rule. The Fluke Rule, that's the one we live by and teach our children to live by, too. But when the cat gets clear of the bag, it's going to say that every boy or girl in America has about the same chance of becoming President of the United States as Williams Jennings Bryan, and he's dead.

WE MAKE OUR OWN OPPORTUNITIES IN THIS WORLD.

Thank you, Sir. Yes, that's true. That is right. I agree with you 100%. But, if that's so, then what right does the Mythfact have in taking credit for it? If you make your own Opportunities in this world, and I believe you do, then we as a country are in about the same league as Pharaoh's Egypt. That's why they chose the pyramid as the symbol on the dollar, because we're about as good in giving out Opportunities as Pharaoh's Egypt. You laugh and snicker. Well, look what Joseph was able to do in Pharaoh's Egypt. Didn't Joseph go from slave directly to head of the government? I hate to be unBusinesslike, but Land of Opportunity has come to seem like just another one of those handy-dandy empty phrases, so empty, in fact, that you can fit Wall Street and Madison Avenue into it and still have room for all fifty states and the protectorate of Puerto Rico.

You see, they set the thing up so that the most desirable things are those that are hard to come by.

YOU KEEP SAYING "THEY." WHO'S "THEY"?

And who are you, Sir, may I ask?

NOBODY IN PARTICULAR.

That's who "they" are. Understand me, I ask you to take what I say with a little humor, with a granary of salt, you might say. This is all just a little Show Business up here. You know what show Business is -- I distract you while my associate picks your pocket. No. I'm only kidding. Oh, my. Look at all those wallets being moved from back to inside pockets.

JUST A PRECAUTION.

Yes. Okay. So, as I was saying, they set the thing up so the things you're supposed to want are the things that are hard to come by. Then they tell you to pull yourself up by your Bootstraps. Then they make a profit selling you Bootstraps. But you're not going anywhere. They reserve the plums for their own kind, while dangling a carrot in front of the Hankering Horde.

When the cat crawls out of the bag, it will tell you that on the American ladder of success the first three rungs are made of sand. You have to be born in Palm Beach or on the fourth rung. That's what they mean when they say the race is to the Swifts, and the Rockefellers, and the DuPonts. It must be wonderful to stand there on that escalator and feel yourself moving up, Up, UP. But a man gets weary trying to work his way up the down escalator.

"Step right up! Step right up! Everybody wins! Just 50 cents, four bits of a dollar. Climb the greased totem pole of Free Enterprise and Opportunity. You can get to the top. Try your luck! Take your chances! You look like a game young man. Show the little lady what you're worth. Ready? Climb the pole! Ha! Ha! Ha! What's the matter, Mister? Ha! Ha! Ha! That's a good sport. Ha! Ha! Ha! Who else wants to try his luck? Step right up! Take your chances! Everybody wins!"

There's only one thing we all want to be in America and that's a million-heir. The problem is you can't try to be a million-heir. You either are one or you're not. Of course, it's true a person can, if he's that one guy a year, turn himself into a millionaire. But that's a horse of a different color. Millionaires can't command the same kind of Respect as million-heirs. And there's not much you can do about that. There's a Society Section and a

Help Wanted Section, and you were born into one or the other. You can change newspapers, but you can't change Sections.

Let me try to clear something up right here and now. Because there's a lot of confusion about just what the Free Enterprise System really is. I'm not sure that I can explain what it is but I'll give it a try. I believe the Free Enterprise System is something like this. If you were born poor, that's your parents' fault. If you grow up poor, that's your parents' fault again. It keeps being your parents' fault until you reach the age of twenty-one. Then it's your fault. That's the Free Enterprise System.

But for the downhearted there is relief, in some form. When that carrot dangling in front of your nose starts to take on a wilted appearance, and not even watering it with your tears every night can put the spring of life back into it, that's when you Muddled Class fellows begin to turn interested eyes to the world of sports. There's a reason you fellows enjoy sports so much. It's because through them you can relieve some of the heartache of stalled Opportunism. Watching athletes running back and forth and up and down relieves the feeling of stalled Opportunity. No more molassified mobility. There's action, movement, knocking guys down, jumping over hurdles. And none of the hurdles are invisible.

The reason Opportunism feels stalled for you Muddled Class fellows is that the game is not being played according to Hoyle. Well, it is, sort of, but there's a catch to it. You Muddled Class fellows are so touched and flattered you've been allowed to play on the same board with the Well-To-Do, you're blinded to the fact that you're playing checkers, but the Well-To-Do are playing caroms.

Each side is playing according to Hoyle, but different games. Caroms, you know, is the game where they use a stick to knock checker pieces all over the place. You Muddled Class fellows are the checker pieces and you're getting knocked all over the board, while at the same time trying very sincerely to carry on with a friendly game of checkers to try to make it across to the other side of the board. You get hit and you know something's not right but you're not sure what to think. You think you saw a stick out of the corner of your eye, but the Well-To-Do keep hiding the stick behind their backs as soon as you turn their way. They're smiling very politely, very toothy smiles. So you're confused. You think it's something *you've* done wrong, some rule you didn't get right. And you keep on playing, trying to get to the other side. It seems so close. Suddenly, Bang! You're hit so hard you go flying clear off the board. As you sail away you yell, "King me!"

That's what I call muddled.

3.

Trialogue 9

500,000,000 Applicants
Jesus's Goat
Is the Lord Your Shepherd?

Nature, I know it means a lot to you to ensure the continuation of our species, but why put the entire responsibility on my shoulders? Why make me the one who must couple with every single nubile female in the world? And could ethnic diversity be so crucial to the survival of our kind that I must personally assist in advancing the DNA of every variety of female on the planet, of every skin shade, of every eye and hair color, on every continent and especially on every island in the Hawaiian Archipelago? Don't you think that's a bit much to ask of just one man?

MY AGENDA
Won't you surrender your pudenda?
It's certainly first thing on my agenda.

Is it flowers I should send her?
O, won't you surrender your pudenda?

Because of the millions of females and thousands of miles involved in my agenda, I have come up with a simple image to help me visualize the global reproductive mission Nature has foisted upon me. Scientists have named the layers of atmosphere that circle the globe from the distant exosphere, down to the thermosphere, the mesosphere, the stratosphere, and finally the troposphere which rises about 10 miles above the earth. To these I add the pudendasphere circling the planet at roughly 2-3 feet above ground.

Who am I kidding? Things are not as simple as that. Nature, it's your fault. You have no sense of economy. With you it's all about safety in numbers. What you lack in efficiency you make up in overproduction. With you there's no such thing as, Get it right the first time. Your way is, Send in 500,000,000 spermatozoa. That's your way. 500,000,000 applicants for one position! Do you call that equal opportunity? Sure, all are free to compete, but for one job? 499,999,999 applicants are going to turn away disappointed. 499,999,999 little channel swimmers all greased up for nothing.

Every one of those 500,000,000 swimmers wants a mate. Nature's mandate is quite clear, Go out there and mate with 500,000,000 females.

Yes, I know -- A journey of 500,000,000 miles begins with one small step. To hell with your Chinese proverbs! In Asia they're a lot more interested in reproduction than we are. This is the U.S.A. Girls are different here. They don't understand the urgency of the situation. Somebody please tell them what's going on around them. I'm being egged on, but they're not being tested. I'm over here on my little life raft of a bed every night sending up flares that no one sees but me. The night sky lights up with hope for one joyful moment then fades back into darkness.

Nature, you don't give a damn what your inefficiency costs me. It took me 500,000,000 individual desires to produce those wigglies and store them down below in a sack for future use. Then you come along like a thief in the night and steal them all away from me. 500,000,000 amphibious personnel carriers destined never to hit the beach. Why? Because you can't tell the difference between a woman and my right hand, usually. What a waste! Nineteen years on this planet and I've done nothing to save the species from extinction. When I see a girl like that brunette with the fuchsia-ribboned pigtails, the thought rises within me that the human species is a good thing, and I want to do my part to preserve it, the sooner the better. When that urge comes over me the thought of our planet unpeopled, the prospect of the earth without my kind walking on top of it, riding bicycles along it, exchanging currencies, forming and disbanding governments, tipping waiters, and tossing baseballs from one part of it to another seems very, very wrong.

. . .

Excuse me, D. C.?
Speak to me, young lady.

WHAT DO YOU SEE IS THE DIFFERENCE BETWEEN OUR TWO POLITICAL PARTIES? OR DO YOU SEE A DIFFERENCE?

I do. Oh, yes, I do see a difference. They're both parties, of course, but the Republican one is catered. I have to admit, though, that the two parties often feel just about the same. When you come right down to it, they're about equal. As a matter of fact, I think they're just about the best example of Equality we have in this country. Well, you can sense some difference, but it's hard to put your finger on. It's a bit like the difference between a ton of tar and a ton of feathers. Different look, same weight.

Let's admit that, no matter which party is sleeping in the White House, our government seems more or less the same. There's a sameness about it. Well, we do have what they call the Liberals and the Conservatives. A Liberal is a fellow who keeps saying he sees the America of the Future, while a Conservative sees the America of the Future and wants it to stay there. The Conservatives like to think of this country as a sort of new England, a kind of England warmed over.

I believe that our government is naturally conserVAtionist. It cares a lot about protecting for posterity the great American wilderness areas that have escaped civilization, places like the Grand Canyon and Wall Street. Oh, yes, the intersection of Wall Street and Pennsylvania Avenue is the cross we all have to bear. Since we live in the reign of the Business Man, we have to take the kind of government he likes best, which is sort of a glorified Chamber of Commerce.

SO, YOU'D RATHER HAVE A HITLER OR A MUSSOLINI?

No, Sir. Not for a second. But don't it seem strange to you that the highest type of Guide and Leader we could come up with in this great and blessed country of ours is the only man that could make sweet Jesus lose his temper? Jesus was generally rather easy going. He didn't have anything unpleasant to say about the Roman Empire, bad as it was. Never raised his voice against King Herod or Pontius Pilate. He got along pretty well with Pharisees and Sadducees, tax collectors, and women taken in adultery. He was so open-minded he even let a painter be one of his evangelists. Despite all he went through, Jesus stayed pretty much unriled and good-tempered.

But the Business Man got his goat. Imagine, the only man that could get Jesus's goat, changing money in the holy temple of our civilization.

WHAT DO YOU HAVE AGAINST BUSINESS?

Nothing. Nothing at all. The Business Man's no worse or better than the rest of us. He has his place. I'm not taking anything away from a man who runs a good business. We need people to make things and to sell things. But as a spiritual leader for a whole civilization, the Business Man seems to me something of a disappointment. I don't mean to lean too hard on the man. I have a lot of sympathy for him. The poor guy didn't expect to be put in charge of the whole show. I know that. The Business Man has no business running our civilization, and he knows it as well as we do. He's embarrassed by it. Why do you think he has the windows of his limousine painted black?

Some people are okay with the way things are. The Business Man is the perfect Leader for the Muddled Class because, even though they have the annoyance of envying the man, they don't have the nuisance of admiring him. So there's a savings there.

I give the Business Man credit for making the most of his opportunity, and he's doing the best he can to keep things rolling until The Next Thing comes along. We all want what's next, but it hasn't happened yet. Don't worry. It will. Civilization is progressing to a higher and higher plane, or why would so many people keep saying it is?

D. C., DON'T YOU BELIEVE IN PROGRESS?

Progress is whatever's next. It'll feel like Progress to you if your pockets start gaining weight. If they don't, it won't. But don't fret. If things don't suit you the way they are, you can always Declare Your Independence. We are lucky enough to live in America, so that's something that's always available to us.

Don't blame the Business Man. Have a little sympathy. It's nobody fault. It just happened. America started as a business, and it's sort of been that way ever since.

WHAT ABOUT THE PILGRIMS?

Oh, yes, the Pilgrims. The Pilgrims came to this country because of religious persecution. They couldn't do any in England, so they came over here. But they weren't the first ones here, no matter what the Mythfact says. Oh, no, the very first colonists came here to get rich, the first day if possible. You don't hear much about the very first colonists because they were very un-Businesslike, being that they didn't show a profit. You see, way before the Pilgrims, way before the Mayflower, way before Jamestown, Sir Walter Raleigh tried to start the first business in America. We don't hear much about that because the venture didn't turn out so well. Not only did they lose all their employees, they didn't turn a profit. So, we don't hear very much about them.

The first settlement we hear much about is

Jamestown, Virginia. We hear about Jamestown because Jamestown turned a profit. Yes, the first successful business in America was the cigarette and coughing industry at Jamestown, Virginia. The home office back in England actually shipped their employees here to start a gold discovering business, but a depression hit just after they landed, so they discovered tobacco instead.

Tobacco, that nasty weed! Even back then they knew it was a nasty weed. During the first board meeting in Jamestown the local minister stood up to speak against the nasty weed side effects of tobacco and was politely shouted down. A minister ought to know better than to go against the most sacred tenet of American morality: In the long run will it be good for Business? Tobacco is a nasty weed, but there's money in it, so it can't be all bad. Don't bother with the side effects, Reverend. We're talking Business here.

You've got to understand how questions of American morality are settled. If they decide it would be good for Business, whatever it is – it could be the black man or it could be women's rights, or what have you – if they figure it would be good for business in the long run, they pass a law in favor of it, saying, "Ahhuum, a Free People must have the right to ...." But, on the other hand, if they think that, in the long run, it would not be so good for Business, then they pass a law against it, saying, "Ahhuum, it would be against the, ahhuum, the American Way of Life to, ahhuum... ."

EXCUSE, ME, D. C. I'M HERE ON VACATION AND... .

Welcome to Washington.

THANK YOU. WE'RE ENJOYING OURSELVES. I'M HERE ON BUSINESS. I WORK ON WALL STREET AND --

You mean General Motors up a quarter, down a quarter?

YES, THAT'S RIGHT. AND I CAN TELL YOU THERE'S NO BIG CONSPIRACY.

I didn't use the word Conspiracy. I don't like the word. Anyway I never think of the Big Money takeover of our country as a conspiracy. Aren't conspiracies supposed to be secret? But pardon me, Sir. I don't mean to offend you or any man. Folks, I'm not talking about this man's work or the company he works for. I'm talking about History. But you will agree, Sir, that as Wall Street goes, so goes the nation?

YES -- AND NO.

All right. Let's take the Yes part of that for a moment. Ole Tom Paine thought it was against Common Sense for a mighty continent to be governed by an island. Lord, Lord, Lord. Wouldn't he be surprised to hear it's being ruled by a street?

Wall Street. It's a figure of speech, Sir. A figure of speech. But what a figure! I'm talking about History, all the tricky business deals going all the way back to the red man. The red man made the first tricky business deal in America when he sold Manhattan Island to the white man for $24, one of the smartest real estate deals ever made in New York City. The red man walked away from Manhattan Island and still had $24 in his pocket. How does that make the rest of us look? You can't even get a taxicab ride across Manhattan for $24 today.

So many tricky deals, all the dirt that's been swept under the carpet! Let's face it. There are big lumps under the carpet of this great nation. Just look at the map of our country. They first had to sweep things under the carpet west of the original thirteen colonies. That's how that big lump called the Appalachian Mountains got pushed up. So many tricky deals were made after that, they had to shove the dirt waaaaaaaay under. That's when the Rocky Mountains sprang up.

The cat has crawled out of the bag and the cat says this country started as a business, and it's sort of been that way ever since. Even the American Revolution was about money, because back then we didn't want to pay heavy taxes to a distant government that didn't seem to care about our needs! And they say history books don't have a sense of humor.

All this humorous talk about we broke with England because we had much more Liberty to give out, and the British were holding us back, using this country just to make money off of it, and we wanted it so we could dedicate it to The

Proposition. Well, isn't it true that England has always had the jump on us in giving out Liberty and reforms of all kinds? They abolished slavery before we did. And look at women's suffrage. Didn't they allow their women to cast their votes to the wind long before we did? Why, the British are so far ahead of us in their reform thinking, they've even tried to make doctors honest. How many centuries are we behind them in that?

Yes, England was the first to abolish slavery. I hate to mention slavery again, but there's something about it that just keeps cropping up. We would much rather believe that the first Americans came over on the Mayflower for reasons of Freedom and Religion. But the first Slave ship beat the Freedom and Religion ship here by a whole year. That may prove to be the longest year in American history.

Things can get very confusing in our country sometimes. But you can break through the confusion if you keep in mind that America started as a Business and it's kind of been that way ever since. The original colonists set out for America with one thing in mind – to find the El Dorado. I grant you, things have changed some since then. Every American today still wants his El Dorado but nowadays he has to go to General Motors to get it. That's the history of America in a hubcap.

. . .

Sunday morning while my landlady was at church, I sneaked into her bedroom. On her bureau, placed on top of a white doily of her own making, were three framed photos hinged together into a triptych shrine dedicated to the trinity. In the center was FDR. On the left, JFK. On the right, LBJ. I had just enough time to run to the corner store for a red-glass votive candle. I set it down on the doily in front of the trinity and was about to light the wick when I heard her key in the front door. I blew out the match, grabbed the votive candle, and hurried back to my room. I didn't have the heart to hurt her feelings. Poor woman doesn't know any better.

Liberal Democrats have mastered the politics of Good Shepherdism. Do you look to the kindly Shepherds of the People? The shepherd has one intent, to protect his sheep from straying – into freedom. What do you think that sheep hook is for? Do you pretend not to know what becomes of the sheep? Still unwilling to admit where your Good Shepherd is herding you to? Green pastures, to be sure, but that is not the end of the journey. You will be delivered well fed and fat but not to the New Jerusalem. You're on your way to Chicago.

The Good Liberal Shepherd guides his flock to the green pastures of Public Education and the cool waters of Social Entitlements. The herd eats and drinks and fattens, but are the poor lambs wise to what is really going on? No, because they do not know their history! That is how they are kept enthralled. Public Education was instituted not out of benevolence but to keep the herd from learning any more history than can be read on the back of a box of breakfast cereal. Yes, middle class children are force-fed a course in American history in school. But what do they learn of history's great lessons? One only: He who ignores the past is condemned to repeat History 101.

Oh, the Shepherd loves that his publicly educated subjects are trained to do sums. That is useful to the Sales Division, but what do they learn of the majestic laws of mathematics? All they care about is what's on sale. To them the most sublime mathematical expression is the rational number $19.99.

A patient and tolerant upper stratum understands the People's longing for a Benign Master as the mental residue of the ex-peasant, the ex-servant, the ex-slave. What distress they must feel, these members of the herd, when their government refuses to act the Good Shepherd. Yet, should the proprietors of this country ever take their cue from alien politics and come forward, crook in hand, then you may write in the margin of history: This is the beginning of fascism in America. This is the wolf in shepherd's clothing.

The People complain that Republican administrations are heartless. Not so. There is no Father Christmas. Is that callous? Uncle Sam will not compensate you for the lost affection of the father? Is that cruel? But you long for the Benign Master, so you vote for Senator Goodheart. He feels the suffering of the People! A vote for Senator Goodheart is a vote for Love. Tears will flow again in the White House. You will get social legislation! Liberals con the masses by promising to pass ambitious social programs and stick the rich with the bill. And what is the result? Are the poor still with us? Are the rich? The income tax was sold to the people as vengeance against the rich. But look what it has become – a sumptuary law against the vanity and uppitiness of the middle class. The Liberal Democrats tell you they are going to soak the rich and, while you're out celebrating, they've got their arms up to their elbows in your pay envelope.

Have you been flimflammed and fleeced by the Good Shepherd? Serves you right. You didn't read your Bible carefully enough. Jesus said the poor shall always be with you, not just during Republican administrations.

The American people, the pampered darlings of a liberal and benign government, better off than any other people on the planet? One thing is certain. The American workingman gets more *per anum* than in any other place on earth.

Trialogue 10

When an American Prays
Philistia Is Just Over the Hill
A Bull and a Bullfinch

God didn't die. He just turned into a dollar bill. The Constitution says there shall be no establishment of religion, and yet we've made Mammontheism the great American creed. Is the United States of America unConstitutional?

In our religion the wages of sin may be in the millions, but Right makes mite. If it's nonprofit-making it's humane, but if there's money in it it's divine. And it really doesn't matter how you made your money or who had to lose so you could profit. There's no column in the accounting ledger for how the other fellow made out on the deal. And why should there be? Am I my brother's bookkeeper?

This building here behind me, the Jefferson Memorial, the way they designed it only adds to the confusion. These Greek columns make it look like a temple of our religion. All day long I see my fellow citizens going in there thinking it's a bank. They go in expecting to worship and find there aren't any tellers available. All it turns out to be is a memorial to the founder of our democracy.

Thomas Jefferson may have founded America, but it was Alexander Hamilton who founded the Bank of New York. Our religion is not about The Proposition That All Men Are Created Equal. When an American kneels down to pray, he doesn't say, "Lord, make me the equal of my neighbor." He says, "Please, Lord, make me the neighbor of a rich man."

Our religion teaches us to always keep our mind on Higher things, to always want to be Up There. You want to get to that little pyramid Up There on top. You want to get to Heaven on Earth, don't you? Of course, you do. We all do. Heaven on Earth is known by different names across the country. Westchester County, Spring Valley, Beverly Hills. Oh, it's got many names. The name changes from place to place, but they all mean the same thing – what every good American sets his heart on: a manor house with a big iron gate and a guard on the premises to keep the riffraff out. That's Heaven on Earth. That's where we all want to end up.

There are those already in Heaven on Earth who'll be there forever, and they know it. There are those living in hell on earth who'll stay there forever, and they know it. Then there is the great purgatorial Muddled Class. They're Muddled because they don't know whether they're moving up or down. They feel themselves moving but they're never sure in which direction. They strive but they don't know if they'll thrive, just stay alive, or take a nose dive. They're nervous. They're confused. They're Muddled. Still, they love to imagine themselves Up There in a big house with a two-car mirage. Don't you Muddle Class fellows realize it's easier for a camel to pass through the eye of a needle than for a member of the Muddled Class to pass through the iron gate into Heaven on Earth? Wide is the way but narrow is the gate.

Don't listen to the call of our religion's four evangelists – Newspaper, Magazine, Radio, and Television. Television is nothing but an electronic door-to-door salesman. In the old days there used to be this fellow who'd come around and try to spout out some sales pitch before you could slam the door on his bow tie. He'd knock on your door, and you'd open it, and he'd start in with, "GooddayLetMeTakeOneShortMinuteOfYourTime ToDemonstrateThisHandyDandy." You'd shut the door, and that was that.

Today things are different. Today they've got Television, the electronic door-to-door salesman that camps in your living room all day long and pitches and pitches and pitches. And the humorous part is you pay for it yourself.

The four evangelists of our religion will tell you you've got to buy something expensive so you can think of yourself as being Up There. Don't cotton. All you should be worried about are the things that belong to you – your CreatedEqualness and the Opportunity to tell the truth to your children. Shake off the rest. You don't need things that are hard to come by. You don't need a New York specialist. Avoid being finically dressed. Don't cotton. This is America. Declare Your Independence while there's still time. For the End is near. Beware the Day of Judgment, when there shall be the casting out into the Darkness and the weeping and the gnashing of Cadillacs.

. . .

I will have to write the Republican Party Chairman again. We must stop the march of Technology, all those blue-skied prophesies of the glorious future Technology is creating for us. Technology is the answer! The leper is healed. The deaf hear. The dead are raised up. The rich get richer, and the poor have the gospel preached to them – on big screen televisions. Technology may be the wave of the future, but will that wave deposit us on the shore of the Promised Land or crash over our heads with all the force of a new Deluge?

Technology marches on in goose step, and anyone who bares her chest to it is trampled under foot. They think they can squelch us with the taunt, "You can't turn back the clock." Was the Renaissance turning back the clock? Do they really believe in Progress? Which of them will admit that his child is an improvement over him? With no respect for the past and no reverence for the future, Philistia is just over the hill.

The road to Philistia is paved with people with good intentions. Please do not ask me, dear, good-hearted innocents, to sign your petition to bring about the Utopia. Put down your clipboards and your tambourines. Those who try to be a century before their time will end by being a hundred years too early. If you cannot turn back the clock, you certainly cannot force its hands forward. Dame history will not be goosed. Try and she will cuff you mightily.

When I started talking to my landlady about history she turned the television up louder. One of her other boarders tried to tell me that Marx was greater than Jesus because, although Jesus was content to have the poor always with us, Marx set forth the inspiring vision of the end of poverty. That only points up what history has so clearly proven, that, though Marx was the greater religious leader, Jesus was the smarter economist.

. . .

My problem is I'm tumid and shy. I'm half bull, half bullfinch. When it comes to breaking the ice I'm a Titanic failure. I don't know how to talk to girls. The other night at a dance I saw two girls leaning against the wall, talking only to each other. They looked like sisters to me. I told myself to go over and talk to them, friendly like. But taking the first step, the hardwood floor turned to quicksand under my feet. Later, hearing the last dance of the night announced, I finally found my footing and started pinballing my way through the twirling dancers. Only one of the two girls was still leaning against the wall. I figured the other one was dancing. I walked up to the one leaning against the wall and said, "Excuse me, Miss. Would you care to dance?"

She said No, without needing to speak.

I wanted to go back to safety, but the floor turned to concrete around my ankles.

She said, "My feet are tired."

I ventured, "But you haven't danced all night. They couldn't be too tired."

"What are you, my podiatrist?"

I said, "I'd like to be."

She looked straight up to the ceiling.

I said, "I just thought since your sister's dancing that you might also like to dance."

She looked into my face. I took that as encouragement. Then she said, "She's isn't dancing. And she's not my sister. She's my friend. I'm waiting for her." Then she became intensely interested in every single thing in her purse. I thanked her and started walking back across the frozen tundra. Who do I see coming toward me but the other one.

I said, "Your friend's waiting for you."

"What friend?" she inquired.

"That one leaning against the wall looking through her purse."

She said, "That's not my friend. That's my sister."

That's the way it is with me. The Creator saw that it was not good for Man to be alone so he created Woman? I try to stay aloof and above it all but every day I see two or three females who with just a smile could bring my knees to the concrete with a crash, like that one sitting under a fringed beach umbrella, reading a paperback. Why don't I just stroll over to her and casually make myself irresistible? You never know. What is there to be afraid of? She probably speaks English, just like me. I'm sure she breathes air, just like me and puts one foot in front of the other when she walks, just like me. She's unarmed as far as I can tell.

What's wrong with me? Aren't I a man? Hasn't Nature provided me the full panoply of manhood? Actually, I'm a little concerned about my sperm count. I counted them last night and there were three missing.

Trialogue 11

**Leave Your Bootstraps Alone
The Things That Are Caesar's
The Index of Covetability**

When I get pretty good at something I drop it. I put it aside. Happiness, as far as I can tell, is branching out, starting something new, sprouting new shoots, welcoming new life. For example, I like to make up songs. And I came up with a new system of writing music down on paper, a way no one's ever thought of before. Nobody can understand it but me, but that's all right.

It's beginning new things that human beings enjoy. When you were first learning to ice skate, remember how you laughed when you fell down? But did you ever see an accomplished ice skater fall down and enjoy the experience? That's what I'm talking about. Doing the thing right becomes a sort of reputation you've got to live up to when other people are watching. And then you start thinking, Am I doing as well as I'm supposed to be doing?

Muddled Class fellows have to try to get it right because, if they don't, how are they going to have an advantage over the next guy? And, if they're not better than the next guy at something, what are their chances of getting into Heaven on Earth? They think they have to be really good at something so they can command Respect. They're always on the edge of their seat looking for a chance to make a big splash. But tell me this. How are you going to be brilliant all of a sudden? 99.9% of us are ordinary. Way down deep inside we know it but we think if we don't admit it to ourselves maybe nobody else will notice. Or maybe those Up There will see us trying so hard they'll have mercy on us and pull us up to where they are. Fat chance.

Not everybody is called to greatness. The ones who are didn't plan it that way. If you're destined for greatness, greatness will find you, even if you hide. That's the only kind of greatness that counts anyway, when you're just going about your business, and greatness comes and taps you on the shoulder. Look at our Vice President. He didn't waste his time longing and pining to be Vice President of the United States. He just went about his business and greatness fell into his lap.

You don't have to make a big splash. You're not going anywhere. And nobody's watching. Don't picture yourself going back to the old neighborhood in a sleek automobile to strike envy in the hearts of the ones who stayed behind. Don't look to have all the comforts. You don't need a fancy lampshade. You don't need natty clothing. You don't need a New York specialist. Be careful, though, if you do go to one of those New York specialists. They might hold the X-rays up to the light and recommend you undergo a life-savings-adectomy. You don't need that.

Don't go thinking making more money is going to raise your standard of living. Money just brings out the native foolishness in us humans. It doesn't seem to have that effect on dogs or cats, but you put a large denomination in front of a human being, and he does something foolish right off. Give him a roll of bills with strange presidents on them, and straightaway he goes out and buys something everybody but him knows doesn't suit him. You see him the next day on the sidewalk in new shoes that stand out -- and hurt his feet.

Looking back over my life, I find that's been true about me, too. Every time I had a little extra cash I went out and spent it on something that didn't suit me. I'm smart as long as I'm a little poor. I don't mind staying poor because I like myself better when I'm smart.

D. C.?

Yes, young man?

SO WHAT ARE WE SUPPOSED TO DO? SELL ALL WE HAVE AND FOLLOW YOU?

Follow me? By no means. I'm not going anywhere. I'm out here in left field but I like it here. I'm doing just fine. The Lord is my Shepherd. I shall not want. All I'm saying is relax. Ease up a bit. Give your heart a break. Pass up all the shell games and the shall games. Leave your bootstraps alone.

Don't keep thinking you have to be Up There. Branch out. Take a bus. And remember what belongs to you that no man can take away and no rust can tarnish: your CreatedEqualness and the opportunity to tell the truth to your children, and, of course, since we're blessed to live in America, the freedom to Declare Your Independence. Seek out the many things life makes available to you without big denominations changing hands. It sounds impossible, don't it?

I know, what I've been saying doesn't jibe with the Mythfacts, but I thought I'd let the cat out of the bag just for a minute. It's good for the lungs to crawl out of the bag once in a while and take a deep breath. We can turn around and go right back in again. So there's no harm done. Believe everything they tell you but, now and then, step out of the bag for a little fresh air. Stretch out. Branch out. Write a book. Show it to your friends. If you don't have friends, show it to your dog. If she sniffs it and walks away, publish it. It doesn't really matter. You're not going anywhere. Down in front. Relax. Give your heart a break. Have a child and tell her the truth.

And that odd fellow, the one marching so badly out of step. Don't be too hard on him. He might be marching to the beat of a different drummer. Or maybe he's got a rock in his shoe. Have a little sympathy.

D. C.?

Yes, Miss?

DO YOU HAVE ANY CHILDREN?

Many, of both denominations, and many grands. I like to think of all of you as my children, too. I do believe I'm old enough to be the father of everybody here. When I say, "Tell the truth to your children," I mean tell the truth to each other, too. That's what this nation is for. Freedom of Speech -- that's the beauty of this country. And we have the Constitution to guarantee it. It's our right. If there are enough of us telling the truth to each other, why there's a chance that by sheer force of numbers we're going to come within hailing distance of a version of the truth that works for most all of us. That's called Freedom of Speech. That's called Democracy. We live in a country that Constitutionally guarantees it. Now, Isn't that a wonderful thing?

. . .

Will I ever have a real live woman all to myself? I want a home -- that is, a woman, a bed, and walls around them both. Too many people nowadays think of the marital tie as a slipknot, but I'm old-fashioned. I'm going to find a female who adores me and I'm going to let her go on doing that until she predeceases me. It sounds wonderful. What I can't figure out is why so many couples that seem well suited to each other don't stay together. At one of my parents' parties I overheard two men chatting, Martini glasses held loosely in hand. One of them said to the other, "Half the power of attraction depends on the woman being distant and forbidden. The sexiest part of a woman is the space between her – and you." If that's true, if the honeymooning is over when the honeymoon ends, life isn't worth a plug nickel. Will the only up-and-down in a post-honeymoon bedroom be a fight about whether the window should be up or down? When I marry I'm going to make sure my wife and I both have a neutral corner of the house to retire to. I wonder what the rent is on Versailles.

At that same party I overheard the second man say to the first, after placing the skewered olives from the last of his Martini into his mouth, "My wife treats sex the same way she does jury duty. She does it when asked but wouldn't volunteer for it." Could it be that wives frown on extra-marital sex: once a week is marital, everything else is extra? Do I have to limit myself to committing marriage upon my wife only once a week? Will the cutting edge of desire be blunted on the hearthstone of availability? Will passion slacken, while mere physical intimacy grinds on? Is it possible I'll feel desolate and alone even within the small circle of my acquaintance?

I'd like to think of myself as a virtuoso able to perform *The 1812 Overture* on bedsprings. But will my wife tire of me performing the same song night after night? Will she seek another song, another performer? Will I find myself sitting home alone in that lonely nowhere between tweedledee and cuckoldom?

CLEO
It'll come to this, my dream of bliss.
I'll sit home by the fire
And wait for her, a beaten cur
And dog my own desire.

While in fantasy I depilate
Her breasts with teeth for tweezers
Will Cleopatra be embarged on a watery date
Rendering Antony the things that are Caesar's?

. . .

I'm so sick of hearing about the natural, overwhelming sex drive of the male. We women spend billions of dollars and millions of hours perfuming, deodorizing, covering, uncovering, permanenting, altering, elongating, shortening, darkening, lightening, uplifting, downplaying, posing, posturing, and doing voices. And why? So that the male can recognize a desirable female when he sees one.

Want to see a man's desire peter out? Misplace your pink razor for a while. Forget the address of your hair stylist. Toss those high heels in the river. Forego the plucked eyebrow, the painted lip. Wear what feels comfortable. Use your natural voice, and speak your mind! You'll see a change come over the natural, overwhelming sex drive of the male. He'll jump right out the window, the big oaf.

The male of the species will tell you he has only two states: "I'm coming" and "I'm horny." That's it. That's the range, so he says. He will claim that his sexual prowess is limited only by the orgasmic exhaustion of the female, or the sudden return of her husband. But she had better be pretty! And she had better wear nail polish. And she had better dress in a certain way. And, if she could be persuaded to wear a garter belt and stockings, that might help. But remember to keep the seams straight. And, whatever you do, don't sneeze or express a strong opinion about something. What do you want to do, spoil the illusion?

There is nothing so skittish in all the world as the male erection. Ask any woman. Oh, he will tell you he is rascally oversexed. He will tell you he's a regular Alfred Kinsey. But coming down to cases, we find that sometimes in bed he bids his wife goodnight and turns his back on her, too fatigued from the day's toil to perform. Yet, should a sex pollster nudge him awake, up he sits and gives out that story about his nasty, iddy urges, while his poor wife, who knows better, lets fall her weary head, face first, into the pillow.

The male of the species has made the *idea* of sex into a fetish. He's like the philosopher with the *idea* of Chair-ness. The philosopher can fascinate himself for hours with the idea of Chair-ness, but set an actual chair in front of him, and he doesn't get what you're driving at. The male goes around, so he says, in a state of unquenchable appetite. But no sooner is actual food set before him than we see finicality. We see fastidiousness. We see fussiness to the extreme. Hundreds of women will walk by before a special one catches his eye. Does he respond then to Woman? Put a random sample of Nature's *representative* handiwork before him, and the next generation's chances begin to droop. The woman who brings him to the full length of desire has to be abnormal. She has to be a virtual freak of Nature!

Even if the Beautiful One has been attained, her appeal is gone in a trice. Though you may be the one he says he wants most in the world, his dream girl – wait a while. He then takes a closer look and sees that your calf curves a centimeter this way instead of that. Suddenly some other female begins to look like a dream to him. You set him free. He goes to her. And, lo and behold, before long, he finds that, "Well, ah, gee."

The male of the species has been given no mandate from Nature to mate with Beauty. Nature cares not whether the male unburdens himself on Cleopatra's barge or in a jar of camel rub. It's all one to Nature. Let him stand upon the highest dune, impregnating the open sky, Nature is supremely indifferent.

Nature has not provided the male with an innate sense of Beauty. In certain cultures, weights are suspended from a female's breasts that lack the sagging quality the men of that tribe desire most of all. In some nations long ears that hang down upon the shoulders are objects of male delectation. Until recent times, Chinese males vied for the female whose feet most resembled that of a pig. Deformity itself is Beauty to the males, so long as they agree among themselves to deem it so.

The male is driven by one sole desire, to stifle the desire of other men. The more so-called Beauty the female exhibits, the more chagrin-value she represents for him in his competition with other males. The degree of Beauty is merely the index of covetability and therefore a useful ploy in the game of squelchmanship. A male finds a female sexy in so far as he sees, in possession of her, an opportunity to squelch the desire of rival males. This is the sum total of the natural, overwhelming sex drive of the male, where the female is cast in the role of befeathered kewpie doll in the tawdry carnival of male incivility.

Sex is the battlefield not the issue. Sex can be transporting or an infuriating waste of prime reading time. Sex is sex, but all lust is the lust for power. Yet, note. It is power over other men, not power over the female, that drives the male. No wonder that after the sex act, even with a desirable woman, the male feels strangely disappointed, let down, cheated. I have watched that peculiar sadness rework the man's features as he rolls over and stares up at the ceiling. The first time I observed that phenomenon was in my apartment in Rome. I thought there was something wrong with my ceiling.

As the ancients observed, "Men and roosters are depressed after coition." Why? Because power over the female is not what the male craves, though he never suspects it. He is disappointed not by any fault of the female but because the other males in his group are not present to witness his momentary victory over them. The same is probably true of the rooster.

Trialogue 12

This Barren Autogamy
I'm Staying Right Here
Declare Your Independence

Why is she brushing her hair if she doesn't want me to ravish her? She's not friendly. I can tell from here. If I go up to her she's going to tell me to beat it. I'm tired of beating it. I'll be honest with you, I've been playing the devil's solitaire. I've brought countless imaginary women to screams of ecstasy single-handedly. During this seminal period of youth I feel the need to liquidate my mounting tensions. I can't help it. Sanguine thoughts fill me with desire. I fall asleep in their grip. It's the same old saltwater taffy pull every night. Truth is I'm out of control. I'm wearing my fingerprints down to anonymity. I tried to practice *coitus reservatus* but my partner objected.

Why can't I wait until my wedding night? For that I need a woman, but all I have is this barren autogamy. Maybe one day Miss Right will come along. Maybe one day we'll ride together into the sunset. In the meantime I'll ride my one-in-hand to midnight and sleep's merciful forgetfulness.

. . .

I've tried to explain everything to my landlady. She listens for a time then sits back and tells me that if I'm not happy with this country the way it is I ought to go somewhere else. That's the mentality exactly in this country. Just like doctors, they want to take credit for the healthy ones and bury their mistakes. No. No. No. Charity doth not suffereth long. It is not kind. Charity is puffed up. Charity doth behave unseemly. Charity is easily provoked. Charity thinketh evil, rejoiceth in inequity. Charity beareth not all things, believeth not all things. Charity hath not faith. But, damn it all. Charity endureth.

I'm not going anywhere. I'm staying right here.

. . .

When a situation has got as unConstitutional as it is today in our wonderful country, you have the right to Declare Your Independence and rededicate yourself to The Proposition That All Men Are Created Equal.

I hope all of you -- assembled here before me on the steps of this beautiful Memorial dedicated to my long lost relative -- are ready now to make your Declarations. For I am ready to administer the sacred Oath of Independence. So, my brothers and sisters, please repeat after me --

When in the course of human events.

WHEN IN THE COURSE OF HUMAN --

Wait a minute. Wait a minute. I'm sorry. What I meant was, you wait until I'm done. Then you say it. Okay? Good. Now, listen carefully --

When in the course of human events, it becomes wonderful for a people to dissolve the bands which connect them to an unConstitutional situation and to assume among the Powers of the Earth the Separate and Equal station to which Nature and Nature's God entitle them, it is the Right of each Person to institute a new Self-Government, conceived in Liberty, and, admitting money's poor power to add or subtract, laying the Foundation on such Principles as to them shall seem most likely to effect their Joyful Happiness, after a long Train of Abuses, of which the Caboose is not yet in sight, which evinces and shows up a Design to reduce them under Absolute Despotism, it is their Right, it is their Duty, after patient Sufferance of such things as calling together Legislative Bodies for the sole purpose of fatiguing People into Compliance, dissolving Representative Houses and setting up the House of Representatives, erecting a Multitude of new Offices and Bureaus to harass our People and eat out their Substance and Savings Accounts, rendering the Military superior to the People's authority, or Where Were You The Day We All Voted To Go To War, quartering large bodies of Armed Troops to remind the Well-To-Don't not to, setting up so much Trade with other Parts of the World that it makes the East India Company look like a lemonade stand, imposing burdensome Taxes on us, which we had a Revolution in the first place to throw off, transporting beyond the Seas our sons in uniforms that don't fit, altering fundamentally our original Government, declaring Politicians invested with the Power to legislate for us in all Cases whatsoever, it behooves the People to throw off such Governmentlessness which has abdicated governance among us, has waged war against us, has plundered our Seas, ravaged our Coasts, and made the vacant lot the Last Frontier, and since in every stage of these Oppressions have petitions for Redress been made in most humble Terms, which were answered only by repeated Injury, we declare a Governmentlessness like this to be unfit to Rule over a Free People, and considering that we have reminded them of the Circumstances of our Emigration and Settlement, except that we lied when we said that the Pilgrims were the first ones here, because the Slave ship beat the Freedom of Religion ship here by a whole year, which they have turned into, Give me your tired, your hungry and your poor, and we will give them the Business, not excluding Indians, and being as we have appealed to their native Magnanimity, and conjured them by Ties of our Common Kindred to disavow these Usurpations, and as they have been deaf to the Voice of Justice and other idle threats, we hold them, as we hold the rest of Mankind, and therefore we the Human Beings of the United States of America, God bless her, in General Congress assembled here before me, D. C. Washington, who cannot tell a lie, appealing to the Supreme Judge of the World for the Rectitude of our Intentions, do solemnly Publish and Declare that each one of us is and of Right ought to be Free and Independent, and so we absolve ourselves of all allegiance to the United States of ADmerica, and all political Connection between us is, and ought to be, dissolved, except for once every four years on the first Tuesday in November, which isn't very much anyway, and we Declare ourselves with the full Power to conclude War, levy Peace, let up on

Commerce a little so we can breathe, because we're all dying of Consumption, and to do all other Acts and Things which Independent and Free persons may of right do, and for the support of this Declaration, with a firm Reliance on the Protection of Divine Providence, because it is for us the living to be here dedicated to The Proposition That All Men, Women, and Children, including millionaires, not taxed, Are Created Equal, but it took the Free Enterprise System to separate us out, we do hereby ordain and mutually pledge to each other our entire lives and all its contents and all its meanings and purposes, our possessions, such as they are, our privileges, our titles, our homes, our boats, our cars, our bank accounts, our clothes, our furniture, our toothbrushes, our key chains, our rose gardens, our teddy bears, our arms, our legs, our time, our vision, our bow ties, our monogrammed pajamas, our eyeballs, our skills, our skulls, our silver spoons, our carrots, our socks, our stoves, our minds, our trust, our secret prayers, our private plans, our radios, our overalls, our hammers, our stamp collections, our tractors, our pet ferrets, our businesses, our hammocks, our brains, our Fortunes, and our Sacred Honor to ourselves and our Posterity, and do swear to faithfully execute the office of Human Being of the United States of America, and so, with malice toward none, with charity for all, with firmness in the right, as the newspapers give us to see the right, let us strive to the best of our ability to Declare Our Independence every minute of the day from any Purpose not so Conceived and so Dedicated, so help us God.

Okay, now you say it.

www.ingramcontent.com/pod-product-compliance
Lightning Source LLC
Chambersburg PA
CBHW020616300426
44113CB00007B/666